THE UPANISHADS

You are what your deep, driving desire is.

As your desire is, so is your will.

As your will is, so is your deed.

As your deed is, so is your destiny.

[BRIHADARANYAKA IV.4.5]

CLASSICS OF

INDIAN SPIRITUALITY

❏⋮

The Bhagavad Gita

The Dhammapada

The Upanishads

The Upanishads

Introduced &

Translated by

EKNATH

EASWARAN

Afterword by

Michael N. Nagler

Nilgiri Press

© 1987, 2007 by The Blue Mountain Center of Meditation

All rights reserved. Printed in Canada

Second edition. First printing: July 2007

20 19 18 17 16 15 14 13 12 11 10 9

ISBN : 978–1–58638–021–2

Library of Congress Control Number: 2007927661

Cataloging-in-Publication data: see the last page

Printed on recycled paper

Nilgiri Press is the publishing division of the Blue Mountain
Center of Meditation, a nonprofit organization founded
by Eknath Easwaran in 1961. The Center publishes Eknath
Easwaran's books, videos, and audios, and offers retreats
on his eight-point program of passage meditation.
www.bmcm.org | info@bmcm.org

The Blue Mountain Center of Meditation

Box 256, Tomales, California 94971

Telephone: +1 707 878 2369 | 800 475 2369

◨⁝ *Table of Contents*

The Classics of Indian Spirituality

IMAGINE A VAST HALL IN ANGLO-Saxon England, not long after the passing of King Arthur. It is the dead of winter and a fierce snowstorm rages outside, but a great fire fills the space within the hall with warmth and light. Now and then, a sparrow darts in for refuge from the weather. It appears as if from nowhere, flits about joyfully in the light, and then disappears again, and where it comes from and where it goes next in that stormy darkness, we do not know.

Our lives are like that, suggests an old story in Bede's medieval history of England. We spend our days in the familiar world of our five senses, but what lies beyond that, if anything, we have no idea. Those sparrows are hints of something more outside – a vast world, perhaps, waiting to be explored. But most of us are happy to stay where we are. We may even be a bit afraid to venture into the unknown. What would be the point, we wonder. Why should we leave the world we know?

Yet there are always a few who are not content to spend their lives indoors. Simply knowing there is something unknown beyond their reach makes them acutely restless. They have to see what lies outside – if only, as Mallory said of Everest, "because it's there."

This is true of adventurers of every kind, but especially of those who seek to explore not mountains or jungles but consciousness itself: whose real drive, we might say, is not so much to know the unknown as to know the knower. Such men and women can be found in every age and every culture. While the rest of us stay put, they quietly slip out to see what lies beyond.

Then, so far as we can tell, they disappear. We have no idea where they have gone; we can't even imagine. But every now and then, like friends who have run off to some exotic land, they send back reports: breathless messages describing fantastic adventures, rambling letters about a world beyond ordinary experience, urgent telegrams begging us to come and see. "Look at this view! Isn't it breathtaking? Wish you could see this. Wish you were here."

The works in this set of translations – the Upanishads, the Bhagavad Gita, and the Dhammapada – are among the earliest and most universal of messages like these, sent to inform us that there is more to life than the everyday experience of our senses. The Upanishads are the oldest, so varied that we feel some unknown collectors must have tossed into a jumble all the photos, postcards, and letters from this world that they could find, without any regard for source or circumstance.

Thrown together like this, they form a kind of ecstatic slide show – snapshots of towering peaks of consciousness taken at various times by different observers and dispatched with just the barest kind of explanation. But those who have traveled those heights will recognize the views: "Oh, yes, that's Everest from the northwest – must be late spring. And here we're south, in the full snows of winter."

The Dhammapada, too, is a collection – traditionally, sayings of the Buddha, one of the very greatest of these explorers of consciousness. In this case the messages have been sorted, but not by a scheme that makes sense to us today. Instead of being grouped by theme or topic, they are gathered according to some dominant characteristic like a symbol or metaphor – flowers, birds, a river, the sky – that makes them easy to commit to memory. If the Upanishads are like slides, the Dhammapada seems more like a field guide. This is lore picked up by someone who knows every step of the way through these strange lands. He can't take us there, he explains, but he can show us the way: tell us what to look for, warn about missteps, advise us about detours, tell us what to avoid. Most important, he urges us that it is our destiny as human beings to make this journey ourselves. Everything else is secondary.

And the third of these classics, the Bhagavad Gita, gives us a map and guidebook. It gives a systematic overview of the territory, shows various approaches to the summit with their benefits and pitfalls, offers recommendations, tells us what to pack and what to leave behind. More than either of the others, it gives the sense of a personal guide. It asks and answers the questions that you or I might ask – questions not about philosophy or mysticism, but about how to live effectively in a world of challenge and change. Of these three, it is the Gita that has been my own personal guidebook, just as it was Mahatma Gandhi's.

These three texts are very personal records of a landscape that is both real and universal. Their voices, passionately human, speak directly to you and me. They describe the topography of consciousness itself, which belongs as much to us today as to these largely anonymous seers thousands of years ago. If the landscape seems dark in the light of sense perception, they tell us, it has an illumination of its own, and once our eyes adjust we can see in what Western mystics call this "divine dark" and verify their descriptions for ourselves.

And this world, they insist, is where we belong. This wider field of consciousness is our native land. We are not cabin-dwellers, born to a life cramped and confined; we are meant to explore, to seek, to push the limits of our potential as human beings. The world of the senses is just a base camp: we are meant to be as much at home in consciousness as in the world of physical reality.

This is a message that thrills men and women in every age and culture. It is for such kindred spirits that these texts were originally composed, and it is for them in our own time that

I undertook these translations, in the conviction that they deserve an audience today as much as ever. If these books speak to even a handful of such readers, they will have served their purpose.

ॐ *The Upanishads*

"TOWARD THE MIDPOINT OF LIFE'S way," as Dante says, I reached what proved a crisis. Everything I had lived for – literature, music, writing, good friends, the joys of teaching – had ceased to satisfy. Not that my enjoyment of these things was less; in fact, I had every innocent source of joy the world offered. But I found myself thirsting for something more, much more, without knowing what or why.

I was on a college campus at that time, well trained in the world of books. When I wanted to know what human beings had learned about life and death, I naturally went to the library. There I found myself systematically mining the stacks in areas I had never been interested in before: philosophy, psychology, religion, even the sciences. India was still British in those days, and the books available confirmed what my education had taken for granted: anything worth pursuing was best represented in the records of Western civilization.

A colleague in the psychology department found my name

on the checkout card of a volume by William James and grew suspicious. Everyone likes a chance to play Sherlock Holmes; he did some sleuthing and confronted me. "See here," he said, "you're in English literature, but I find you've been taking home every significant contribution to my field. Just what are you up to?"

How could I tell a distinguished professor that I was searching for meaning in life? I gave him a conspiratorial wink and replied simply, "Something *big!*" But nothing I found appeased the hunger in my heart.

About this time – I no longer remember how – I came across a copy of the Upanishads. I had known they existed, of course, but it had never even occurred to me to look into them. My field was Victorian literature; I expected no more relevance from four-thousand-year-old texts than from *Alice in Wonderland.*

"Take the example of a man who has everything," I read with a start of recognition: "young, healthy, strong, good, and cultured, with all the wealth that earth can offer; let us take this as one measure of joy." The comparison was right from my life. "One hundred times that joy is the joy of the *gandharvas*; but no less joy have those who are illumined."

Gandharvas were pure mythology to me, and what illumination meant I had no idea. But the sublime confidence of this voice, the certitude of something vastly greater than the world offers, poured like sunlight into a long-dark room:

Hear, O children of immortal bliss!
You are born to be united with the Lord.
Follow the path of the illumined ones,
And be united with the Lord of Life.

I read on. Image after image arrested me: awe-inspiring images, scarcely understood but pregnant with promised meaning, which caught at my heart as a familiar voice tugs at the edge of awareness when you are struggling to wake up:

 As a great fish swims between the banks of a river as it likes, so does the shining Self move between the states of dreaming and waking.

As an eagle, weary after soaring in the sky, folds its wings and flies down to rest in its nest, so does the shining Self enter the state of dreamless sleep, where one is free from all desires. The Self is free from desire, free from evil, free from fear . . .

Like strangers in an unfamiliar country walking every day over a buried treasure, day by day we enter that Self while in deep sleep but never know it, carried away by what is false.

Day and night cannot cross that bridge, nor old age, nor death, nor grief, nor evil or good deeds. All evils turn back there, unable to cross; evil comes not into this world of Brahman. One who crosses by this bridge, if blind, is blind no more; if hurt, ceases to be hurt; if in sorrow, ceases sorrowing. At this boundary night itself becomes day: night comes not into the world of Reality. . . .

And, finally, simple words that exploded in my conscious-ness, throwing light around them like a flare: "There is no joy in the finite; there is joy only in the Infinite."

I too had been walking every day over buried treasure and never guessed. Like the man in the Hasidic fable, I had been seeking everywhere what lay in my own home.

In this way I discovered the Upanishads, and quickly found myself committed to the practice of meditation.

Today, after more than forty years of study, these texts are written on my heart; I am familiar with every word. Yet they never fail to surprise me. With each reading I feel I am setting out on a sea so deep and vast that one can never reach its end. In the years since then I have read widely in world mysticism, and often found the ideas of the Upanishads repeated in the idi-oms of other religions. I found, too, more practical guides; my own, following the inspiration of Mahatma Gandhi, became the Bhagavad Gita. But nowhere else have I seen such a pure, lofty, heady distillation of spiritual wisdom as in the Upani-shads, which seem to come to us from the very dawn of time.

THE VEDAS AND THE UPANISHADS

Around 2000 B.C., scholars believe, groups of Indo-European-speaking peoples calling themselves *arya*, or noble, began to enter the Indian subcontinent through the Hindu Kush. There, in the Indus river valley, they found a civilization already a thousand years old, thriving and advanced in technology and trade. From the fusion of these two cultures, the Aryan and the Indus Valley, Indian civilization was born.

The Aryans brought their gods and a religion based on ritual sacrifice, with lyrical, life-affirming hymns meant for incantation in an ancient form of Sanskrit. These hymns, dating from perhaps 1500 B.C., reveal an intimate, almost mystical bond between worshipper and environment, a simultaneous sense of awe and kinship with the spirit that dwells in all things. Even in translation they have a compelling beauty. They worship natural forces and the elemental powers of life: sun and wind, storm and rain, dawn and night, earth and heaven, fire and offering.

These powers are the *devas,* gods and goddesses sometimes recognizable in other religions of Aryan origin. In the hymns they seem very near, present before us in the forms and forces of the natural world. Fire is Agni, worshipped as the actual fire on the hearth or altar and as the divine priest who carries offerings to the gods. The storm is Indra, leader of the gods and lord of war and thunder, who rides into battle on his swift chariot to fight the dragon-demon of the sky or the enemies of the Aryan hosts. The wind is Vayu. Night is Ratri and the dawn is Usha, loveliest and most luminous of the goddesses.

The sun is Surya, who rides his chariot across the sky, or Savitri, the giver of life. And death is Yama, the first being to die and thereby first in the underworld.

Throughout the hymns of this early age there is little or no trace of fear. The forces of life are approached with loving reverence and awe, as allies of humanity in a world that is essentially friendly so long as its secrets are understood. And although the devas must once have been a pantheon of separate deities, it seems clear even in the earliest hymns that one Supreme Being is being worshipped in different aspects. "Truth is one," one hymn proclaims, "though the wise call it by many names."

These poetic outpourings of worship served as liturgy in a complicated ritual religion centering around symbolic sacrifice: the holy words of the hymns were chanted as offerings were poured into the fire. Such ceremonies were performed for the *kshatriyas,* the warriors and rulers of the clans, by priests called brahmins, whose function in society was to preserve rites already too ancient to be understood.

As time passed, brahmins produced commentaries to explain the meaning of these ancient rites. Hymns and commentaries together became a sacred heritage passed from generation to generation. These are the Vedas, India's scriptures. *Veda* comes from the root *vid,* "to know": the Vedas are revealed knowledge, given to humanity, according to the orthodox view, at the very dawn of time. They exist in four collections, each associated with its own family tradition: Rig, Sama, Yajur, and Atharva, with the Rig Veda easily the oldest. The first and largest part of each collection, called *karma kanda*, preserves the hymns and philosophical interpretations of rituals used in Hindu worship to this day.

Yet this is only a part of Hinduism, and the least universal. The second part of each Veda, called *jnana kanda*, concerns not ritual but wisdom: what life is about; what death means; what the human being is, and the nature of the Godhead that sustains us; in a word, the burning questions that men and women have asked in every age. The ritual sections of the Vedas define the religion of a particular culture; but the second part, the Upanishads, is universal, as relevant to the world today as it was to India five thousand years ago.

What is an Upanishad? Etymologically the word suggests "sitting down near": that is, at the feet of an illumined teacher in an intimate session of spiritual instruction, as aspirants still do in India today. Often the teacher is one who has retired from worldly life to an ashram or "forest academy" along the banks of the upper Ganges, to live with students as a family, teaching in question-and-answer sessions and by example in daily living. Other settings are explicitly dramatic: a wife asks her husband about immortality, a king seeks instruction from an illumined sage; one teenage boy is taught by Death himself, another by fire, beasts, and birds. Sometimes these sages are women, and some of the men who come for spiritual instruction are kings.

The Upanishads record such sessions, but they have little in common with philosophical dialogue like Plato's. They record the inspired teachings of men and women for whom the transcendent Reality called God was more real than the world reported to them by their senses. Their purpose is not so much instruction as inspiration: they are meant to be expounded by an illumined teacher from the basis of personal experience. And although we speak of them together as a body, the Upanishads are not parts of a whole like chapters in a book. Each is complete in itself, an ecstatic snapshot of transcendent Reality.

When these texts were composed, or who composed them, no one knows. The sages who gave them to us did not care to leave their names: the truths they set down were eternal, and the identity of those who arranged the words irrelevant. We do not even know how many once existed. For the last thousand years, however, ten have been considered the "principal Upanishads" on the authority of Shankara, a towering eighth-century mystic who reawakened India to its spiritual heritage. These ten Upanishads are offered in this book, along with one other of equal importance and great beauty, the Shvetashvatara. Four of the so-called Yoga

Upanishads have been added to represent later traditions.

Fascinatingly, although the Upanishads are attached to the Vedas, they seem to come from an altogether different world. Though harmonious enough in their Vedic setting, they have no need of it and make surprisingly little reference to it; they stand on their own authority. Rituals, the basis of Vedic religion, are all but ignored. And although the Vedic gods appear throughout, they are not so much numinous beings as aspects of a single underlying power called Brahman, which pervades creation yet transcends it completely. This idea of a supreme Godhead is the very essence of the Upanishads; yet, remarkably, the word *brahman* in this sense does not appear in the hymn portion of the Rig Veda at all.

These are signs of a crucial difference in perspective. The rest of the Vedas, like other great scriptures, look outward in reverence and awe of the phenomenal world. The Upanishads look inward, finding the powers of nature only an expression of the more awe-inspiring powers of human consciousness.

If mysticism can arise in any age, there is no reason to suppose that the Upanishads are a late flowering of Vedic thought. They may represent an independent tributary into the broad river of the Vedas. Some age-old elements of Hindu faith can be traced more easily to the pre-Aryan Indus Valley civilization than to Vedic ritual, and archaeologists have uncovered there a striking stone image which a Hindu villager today would identify without hesitation as Shiva, Lord of Yoga, seated in meditation, suggesting that the disciplines of mysticism might have been practiced in India before the Aryans arrived.

All this is speculation, of course. But the fact remains that the Upanishads, while fully at home in the Vedas, offer a very different vision of what religion means. They tell us that there is a Reality underlying life which rituals cannot reach, next to which the things we see and touch in everyday life are shadows. They teach that this Reality is the essence of every created thing, and the same Reality is our real Self, so that each of us is one with the power that created and sustains the universe. And, finally, they testify that this oneness can be realized directly, without the mediation of priests or rituals or any of the structures of organized religion, not after death but in this life, and that this is the purpose for which each of us has been born and the goal toward which evolution moves. They teach, in sum, the basic principles of what Aldous Huxley has called the Perennial Philosophy, which is the wellspring of all religious faith.

THE SUPREME SCIENCE

Yet the Upanishads are not philosophy. They do not explain or develop a line of argument. They are *darshana,* "something seen," and the student to whom they were taught was expected not only to listen to the words but to *realize* them: that is, to make their truths an integral part of character, conduct, and consciousness.

Despite their idyllic setting, then, these intimate sessions were not casual Ivy League seminars on the commons green. Students were there because they were prepared to devote a good measure of their lives – the traditional period was twelve years – to this unique kind of higher education, where study meant not reading books but a complete, strenuous reordering of one's life, training the mind and senses with the dedication required of an Olympic athlete.

In this context, it is clear that the questions the Upanishads record – "What happens at death? What makes my hand move, my eyes see, my mind think? Does life have a purpose, or is it governed by chance?" – were not asked out of mere curiosity. They show a burning desire to *know*, to find central principles which make sense of the world we live in. The students gathered in these forest academies were engaged in a colossal gamble: that they could learn to apprehend directly a Reality beyond ordinary knowing, of whose very existence they had no assurance except the example of their teacher and the promise of the scriptures. It is no wonder that such students were rigorously tested before being accepted – tested not merely for intelligence but for singleness of purpose and strength of will. What is remarkable is that candidates were found at all. As the Katha Upanishad says, only a few even hear these truths; of those who hear, only a few understand, and of those only a handful attain the goal.

This fervent desire to know is the motivation behind all science, so we should not be surprised to find in Vedic India the beginnings of a potent scientific tradition. By the Christian era it would be in full flower: Indian mathematicians would have developed modern numerals, the decimal place system, zero, and basic algebra and trigonometry; surgeons would be performing operations as sophisticated as cataract surgery and caesarian section. But the roots of this scientific spirit are in the Vedas. "All science," Aldous Huxley wrote, ". . . is the reduction of multiplicities to unities." Nothing is more characteristic of Indian thought. The Vedic hymns are steeped in the conviction of *rita*, an order that pervades creation and is reflected in each part – a oneness to which all diversity can be referred.

From this conviction follows a highly sophisticated notion: a law of nature must apply uniformly and universally. In renaissance Europe, this realization led to the birth of classical physics. In ancient India it had equally profound consequences. While the rest of Vedic India was studying the natural world, more or less in line with other scientifically precocious civilizations such as Greece and China, the forest civilization of the

Upanishads took a turn unparalleled in the history of science. It focused on the medium of knowing: the mind.

The sages of the Upanishads show a unique preoccupation with states of consciousness. They observed dreams and the state of dreamless sleep and asked what is "known" in each, and what faculty could be said to be the knower. What exactly is the difference between a dream and waking experience? What happens to the sense of "I" in dreamless sleep? And they sought invariants: in the constantly changing flow of human experience, is there anything that remains the same? In the constantly changing flow of thought, is there an observer who remains the same? Is there any thread of continuity, some level of reality higher than waking, in which these states of mind cohere?

These are the kinds of questions the sages asked, but for some reason they did not stop with debating them. They became absorbed in the discovery that as concentration deepens, the mind actually passes through the states of consciousness being inquired about. And in concentrating on consciousness itself – "Who is the knower?" – they found they could separate strata of the mind and observe its workings as objectively as a botanist observes a flower.

The significance of this discovery cannot be exaggerated. Since consciousness is the field of all human activity, outward as well as inner – experience, action, imagination, knowledge, love – a science of consciousness holds out the promise of central principles that unify all of life. "By knowing one piece of gold," the Upanishads observed, "all things made out of gold are known: they differ only in name and form, while the stuff of which all are made is gold." And they asked, "What is that one by knowing which we can know the nature of everything else?" They found the answer in consciousness. Its study was called *brahmavidya*, which means both "the supreme science" and "the science of the Supreme."

It is important to understand that brahmavidya is not intellectual study. The intellect was given full training in these forest academies, but brahmavidya is not psychology or philosophy. It is, in a sense, a lab science: the mind is both object and laboratory. Attention is trained inward, on itself, through a discipline the Upanishads call *nididhyasana*: meditation.

The word *meditation* is used in so many different ways that I want to be clear before going further. Meditation here is not reflection or any other kind of discursive thinking. It is pure concentration: training the mind to dwell on an interior focus without wandering, until it becomes absorbed in the object of its contemplation. But absorption does not mean unconsciousness. The outside world may be forgotten, but meditation is a state of intense inner wakefulness.

This is not an exotic experience. Even at the university I had students whose concentration was so good that when they were studying, they would be oblivious to what was going on around them. If I called them by name, they might not even hear. Meditation is closely related to this kind of absorption, but the focus is not something external that one looks at or listens to, such as a microscope slide or lecture. It is consciousness itself, which means that *all* the senses close down.

Similarly, although meditation is not discursive thinking, it is not the same as intuition or imagination. We read about the concentration of great artists, writers, and poets who, by focusing on the impressions the world presents, or on a block of formless stone, seize what fits a unifying vision in their mind and fashion some way to share it. Brahmavidya has affinities with this way of knowing also, which is not so different from the intuition of a great scientist. But brahmavidya is not concerned with the insights that come from concentrating on a particular part of life; it is concerned with how concentration yields insight at all. Observing what happens as concentration deepens, the sages of the Upanishads learned to make a science and art and craft of insight – something that could be mastered and then taught to others, as a painting master in the Renaissance might take a gifted student to live as part of his family and absorb his art.

Recently I read a penetrating remark by William James, the great American psychologist, which spells out the significance of this skill: "The faculty of voluntarily bringing back a wandering attention over and over again is the very root of judgment, character and will. An education which should include this faculty would be the education *par excellence*." James was not guessing. He tried to teach himself this skill, at least as it applies to everyday affairs, and he succeeded well enough to lift himself out of a life-threatening depression. In this pivotal achievement he grasped the connection between training the mind and mastering life. He would have acclaimed the forest universities of the Upanishads, which built their curricula on this connection: "education *par excellence*" is almost a literal translation of *brahmavidya*.

Brahmavidya and conventional science both begin when a person finds that the world of sense impressions, so transient and superficial, is not enough in itself to satisfy the desire for meaning. Then one begins to stand back a little from the senses and look below the surface show of life in search of underlying connections. But the sages of the Upanishads wanted more than explanations of the outside world. They sought principles that would unify and explain the whole of human experience: including, at the same time, the world within the mind. If the observer observes through the medium of consciousness, and the world too is observed in consciousness, should not the same laws apply to both?

In the Brihadaranyaka Upanishad there is a long, haunting exposition of the states of mind the sages explored. They called them waking, dreaming, and dreamless sleep, but somehow they had made the brilliant observation that these are not merely alternate states which a person slips in and out of every day. They also represent layers of awareness, concurrent strata lying at different depths in the conscious and unconscious mind.

In dreaming, the Upanishad observes, we leave one world and enter another. "In that dream world there are no chariots, no animals to draw them, no roads to ride on, but one makes chariots and animals and roads oneself from the impressions of past experience." And then the leap of insight: "Everyone experiences this, but no one knows the experiencer." What is the same in both worlds, the observer both of waking experience and of dreams? It cannot be the body, for in dreams it detaches itself from the body and senses and creates its own experiences – experiences which can be as real, in terms of physiological reactions, as those of waking life. "When a man dreams that he is being killed or chased by an elephant, or that he is falling into a well, he experiences the same fear that he would in the waking state": his heart races, blood pressure rises, stress hormones pour into the body, just as if the event were real. Dream and waking are made of the same stuff, and as far as the nervous system is concerned, both kinds of experience are real.

When we wake up from a dream, then, we do not pass from

unreality to reality; we pass from a lower level of reality to a higher one. Havelock Ellis, the psychologist who devoted his life to the study of sex, observed, "Dreams are real as long as they last. Can we say more of life?"

If waking experience is impermanent, should there not be something abiding, something real, to support it? Might it not be possible to wake up into a higher state, a level of reality above this world of constantly changing sensory impressions? The sages found a clue: in dreamless sleep, the observing self detaches itself not only from the body but from the mind. "As a tethered bird grows tired of flying about in vain to find a place of rest and settles down at last on its own perch, so the mind," like the body, "settles down to rest" in dreamless sleep – an observation in harmony with current research, which suggests that in this state the autonomic nervous system is repaired.

This still world is always present in the depths of the mind. It is the deepest, most universal layer of the unconscious. Wake up in this state, the Upanishads say, and you will be who you truly are, free from the conditioning of body and mind in a world unbounded by the limitations of time, space, and causality.

Wake up in the very depths of the unconscious, when thought itself has ceased? The language makes no more sense than a map of some other dimension. Here the Upanishads are like pages from ancient logbooks, recording journeys of exploration into the uncharted waters of the world within. If Freud's limited glimpses of the unconscious can have had such an impact on civilization, the sages who mapped the mind three thousand years earlier must rank with the greatest explorers in history.

Yet this is dangerous territory. We know what forces can buffet us in the dream world, and that is only the foothills of the dark ranges of the mind, where fear, passion, egotism, and desire so easily sweep aside the will. One of Hopkins' "dark sonnets" hints at the dangers of these realms:

> O the mind, mind has mountains; cliffs of fall
> Frightful, sheer, no-man-fathomed. Hold them cheap
> May, who never hung there . . .

The Katha Upanishad would agree. In famous words it warns that the ascent to the summit of consciousness is not for the timid: "Sharp like a razor's edge, the sages say, is the path to Reality, difficult to traverse." Nothing in the Upanishads is more vital than the relationship between student and guide. The spiritual teacher must know every inch of the way, every danger and pitfall, and not from books or maps or hearsay. He must have traveled it himself, from the foothills to the highest peaks. And he must have managed to get back down again, to be able to relate to students with humanity and compassion. Not everyone who attains Self-realization can make a reliable guide. I have been saying "he," but this is not a role for men alone. My own teacher is my mother's mother.

This spiritual ascent is so fraught with challenge that we can see why the sages took their students young. Exploring the unconscious requires the daring of the years between twelve and twenty, when if someone says "Don't try to climb that peak, you'll get hurt," you immediately go and start climbing. As we grow older, something changes; we start listening to those cautionary voices and say we are learning prudence. So it is no accident that the hero of the Katha Upanishad is a teenager. The message of the Katha, which echoes throughout the Upanishads, is to dare like a teenager: to reach for the highest you can conceive with everything you have, and never count the cost.

What makes a human being dare the impossible? What fires the will when we glimpse something never done before and a wild urge surges up to cry, "Then let's do it"? Here in San Francisco a young woman blind from birth decides to sail alone across the Pacific and succeeds; I can't imagine getting as far as Alcatraz. Mountaineers decide that it is not enough merely to climb Mount Everest; they have to climb it alone, take no oxygen, and choose the most difficult ascent. And just a few months ago a man and woman mortgaged their future to put together a fragile plane with a cockpit smaller than a phone booth, so they could fly around the world without a stop. We ask, "Why did you do it?" And the pilot of the *Voyager* can only reply with a shrug, "Just for the hell of it." He can give no better reason, yet everyone understands.

The sages would say similarly, "Just for the heaven of it." Just to reach for the highest. Human beings cannot live without challenge. We cannot live without meaning. Everything ever achieved we owe to this inexplicable urge to reach beyond our grasp, do the impossible, know the unknown. The Upanishads would say this urge is part of our evolutionary heritage, given to us for the ultimate adventure: to discover for certain who we are, what the universe is, and what is the significance of the brief drama of life and death we play out against the backdrop of eternity.

In haunting words, the Brihadaranyaka declares:

> You are what your deep, driving desire is.
> As your desire is, so is your will.
> As your will is, so is your deed.
> As your deed is, so is your destiny.
>
> (Brihadaranyaka IV.4.5)

In the end, all achievement is powered by desire. Each of us has millions of desires, from big to trivial, packed with a certain measure of will to get that desire fulfilled. Imagine how much power is latent in the human personality! With just a fraction of that potential, young Alexander conquered continents, Rutan and Yaeger flew *Voyager* around the world, Einstein penetrated the heart of the universe. If a person could fuse *all* human desires, direct them like a laser, what would be beyond reach?

This stupendous aim is the basis of brahmavidya. Every desire for fulfillment in the world outside is recalled – not stifled or repressed, but consolidated in one overriding desire for Self-realization. Contrary to a common misunderstanding, there is nothing drab or life-denying about this apparent reversal of human nature. The passion it requires is not different from what a great ballet dancer or gymnast or musician demands. In Sanskrit this ardent, one-pointed, self-transcending passion is called *tapas*, and the Vedas revere it as an unsurpassable creative force. From the tapas of God, the Rig Veda says, the cosmos itself was born.

What daring the sages of the Upanishads conceal in their anonymity! It is no wonder that so many came from the warrior caste. There was nothing world-denying when these sages-to-be left their courts and cities for the Ganges forests. World-weariness cannot generate tapas. They yearned to know life at its core, to know it and master it, and that meant to master every current of the mind.

Sex, of course, is the most powerful desire most people have, and therefore the richest source of personal energy. *Brahmacharya*, self-control in thought and action, was a prerequisite in these forest academies. But this was not suppression or repression. Sexual desire, like everything else in the Upanishads, is only partly physical. Essentially it is a spiritual force – pure, high-octane creative energy – and brahmacharya means its transformation. *Tapas*, the sages say, becomes *tejas*: the radiant splendor of personality that shows itself in love, compassion, creative action, and a melting tenderness which draws all hearts.

Nothing is lost in this transformation. It is clear in the Upanishads that sex is sacred, and ashram graduates often went back into the world to take up the responsibilities of family life. But they did so in freedom. Free from conditioning, they had a choice in everything they did, even in what they thought. Their ideal was not to retire from the world but to live in it selflessly, with senses and passions completely under control. This freedom is the hallmark of the Upanishads, and nothing better suits the life-affirming spirit of the Vedas.

ATMAN & BRAHMAN

In meditation, as the mind settles down to dwell on a single focus, attention begins to flow in a smooth, unbroken stream, like oil poured from one container to another. As this happens, attention naturally retreats from other channels. The ears, for example, still function, but you do not hear; attention is no longer connected with the organs of hearing.

When concentration is profound, there are moments when you forget the body entirely. This experience quietly dissolves physical identification. The body becomes like a comfortable jacket: you wear it easily, and in meditation you can unbutton and loosen it until it scarcely weighs on you at all.

Eventually there comes a time when you get up from meditation and *know* that your body is not you. This is not an intellectual understanding. Even in the unconscious the nexus is cut, which means there are sure signs in health and behavior: no physical craving will be able to dictate to you, and any compulsion to fulfill emotional needs through physical activities will vanish. Most important, you lose your fear of death. You know with certitude that death is not the end, and that you will not die when the body dies.

The Taittiriya Upanishad says that the body is the first of many layers that surround the human personality, each less physical than the one before. These are, roughly, components of what we call "mind": the senses, emotions, intellect, will. As awareness is withdrawn from these layers of consciousness one by one, the sages gradually made another astonishing discovery: the powers of the mind have no life of their own. The mind is not conscious; it is only an instrument of consciousness – or, in different metaphors, a process, a complex field of forces. Yet when awareness is withdrawn from the mind, *you* remain aware. When this happens you realize you are not the mind, any more than you are the physical body.

When awareness has been consolidated even beyond the mind, little remains except the awareness of "I." Concentration is so profound that the mind-process has almost come to a standstill. Space is gone, and time so attenuated that it scarcely seems real. This is a taste of *shanti*, "the peace that passeth understanding," invoked at the end of every Upanishad as a reminder of this sublime state. You rest in meditation in what the Taittiriya Upanishad calls the "body of joy," a silent, ethereal inner realm at the threshold of pure being.

For a long while it may seem that there is nothing stirring in this still world, so deep in consciousness that the phenomena of the surface seem as remote as a childhood dream. But gradually you become aware of the presence of something vast, intimately your own but not at all the finite, limited self you had been calling "I."

All that divides us from the sea of infinite consciousness at this point is a thin envelope of personal identity. That envelope cannot be removed by any amount of will; the "I" cannot erase itself. Yet, abruptly, it does vanish. In the climax of meditation the barrier of individuality disappears, dissolving in a sea of pure, undifferentiated awareness.

This state the Upanishads call *turiya* – literally "the fourth," for it lies beyond waking, dreaming, and dreamless sleep. Turiya, the Upanishads say, is waking up in dreamless sleep: in the very depths of the unconscious, where one is aware of neither body nor mind. In later Hindu thought this awakening will receive more familiar names: *samadhi*, "complete absorption"; *moksha*, "liberation" or "release," for it brings freedom from all conditioning and the limitations of time and space.

What remains when every trace of individuality is removed? We can call it pure being, for it is in differentiating this unity that created things acquire their name and form. The sages called it Brahman, from the root *brih*, "to expand." Brahman is the irreducible ground of existence, the essence of every thing – of the earth and sun and all creatures, of gods and human beings, of every power of life.

Simultaneous with this discovery comes another: this unitary awareness is also the ground of one's own being, the core of personality. This divine ground the Upanishads call simply *Atman*, "the Self" – spelled with a capital to distinguish it from the individual personality. In the unitive state the Self is *seen* to be one, the same in everyone. This is not a reasoned conclusion; it is something experienced at the very center of one's being, an inalienable fact. In all persons, all creatures, the Self is the innermost essence. And it is identical with Brahman: our real Self is not different from the ultimate Reality called God.

This tremendous equation – "the Self is Brahman" – is the central discovery of the Upanishads. Its most famous formulation is one of the *mahavakyas* or "great formulae": *Tat tvam asi*, "You are That." "That" is the characteristic way the

Upanishads point to a Reality that cannot be described; and "you," of course, is not the petty, finite personality, but that pure consciousness "which makes the eye see and the mind think": the Self.

In this absorption there is no time, no space, no causality. These are forms imposed by the mind, and the mind is still. Nor is there awareness of any object; even the thought of "I" has dissolved. Yet awareness remains: *chit*, pure, undifferentiated consciousness, beyond the division of observer and observed. When the mind-process starts up again, as it must, and we slip back into body and personality, the multiplicity of the perceptual world will unfold as a seed bursts into a tree.

Astrophysicists use similar language when they talk about creation. All the matter in the universe must have been present in that "primeval atom," supercondensed to an unbelievable degree. In such a state, matter would no longer be possible as matter. It would be stripped down to pure energy, and energy itself would be raw and undifferentiated; variations like gravity and light would not have emerged. Time would not yet be real, for there can be no time before zero; neither would space make sense in the context of a question like, "What was there before the Big Bang?" Physicists reply, with Gertrude Stein, "There's no 'there' there. There's no 'then' then." Space and time, matter and energy, sprung into existence at the moment of creation; "before" that moment the concepts do not apply.

The sages would find all this a perfect metaphor for the unitive state. In samadhi, reality is condensed into pure potential, without dimensions, without time, without any differentiation. Physicists do not say there was nothing before the Big Bang; they say everything came from that, and nothing more can be said. Similarly, samadhi is not emptiness but *purnata*: plenitude, complete fullness. The whole of reality is there, inner as well as outer: not only matter and energy but all time, space, causality, and states of consciousness.

That fullness the Upanishads call *sat*: absolute reality, in which all of creation is implicit as an organism is implicit in DNA, or a tree in a tiny seed.

The joy of this state cannot be described. This is *ananda*: pure, limitless, unconditioned joy. The individual personality dissolves like salt in a sea of joy, merges in it like a river, rejoices like a fish in an ocean of bliss. "As a man in the arms of his beloved," says the Brihadaranyaka daringly, "is not aware of what is without and what within, so one in union with the Self is not aware of what is without and what within, for in that state all desires are fulfilled." And what other scripture would cap such an image with a pun? "*Apta-kamam atma-kamam akamam rupam*: That is his real form, where he is free from all desires because all his desires are fulfilled; for the Self is all our desire."

Nothing less can satisfy the human heart. "There is no joy in the finite; there is joy only in the infinite." That is the message of the Upanishads. The infinite – free, unbounded, full of joy – is our native state. We have fallen from that state and seek it everywhere: every human activity is an attempt to fill this void. But as long as we try to fill it from outside ourselves, we are making demands on life which life cannot fulfill. Finite things can never appease an infinite hunger. Nothing can satisfy us but reunion with our real Self, which the Upanishads say is *sat-chit-ananda*: absolute reality, pure awareness, unconditioned joy.

THE DISCOVERIES

What can be said of a state of being in which even the separate observer disappears? "Words turn back frightened," the Upanishads say: every attempt to explain produces contradictions and inconsistencies. But the sages of the Upanishads must have longed so ardently to communicate that they *had* to try, even if the picture was doomed to be inadequate.

Some time ago I remember watching footage of how the *Titanic* was discovered – two and a half miles below the surface of the ocean, far beyond depths that light can penetrate, where the sheer weight of the sea would crush a human being. Scientists designed a twelve-foot robot called *Argo* and lowered it little by little through those black waters right to the ocean floor. At those blind depths, probing with cameras and sonar, they began to piece together a vivid picture of a world no one could have seen before. The video seemed to take us through doors that had not been opened for seventy years, down that famous staircase into a silent crystal ballroom uncorrupted by time – eerie, disjointed shots of a lightless landscape. That is how I think of the Upanishads, probing depths where individuality itself dissolves and sending up pictures of treasures sunk in the seabed of the unconscious.

What do they report? They tell us, first, that whatever we are, whatever we may have done, there is in each of us an inalienable Self that is divine:

> As the sun, who is the eye of the world,
> Cannot be tainted by the defects in our eyes
> Nor by the objects it looks on,
> So the one Self, dwelling in all, cannot
> Be tainted by the evils of the world.
> For this Self transcends all!
>
> (Katha II.2.11)

They remind us that love is the first and last commandment of this realization, for the same Self dwells in all:

> As the same fire assumes different shapes
> When it consumes objects differing in shape,
> So does the one Self take the shape
> Of every creature in whom he is present.
>
> (Katha II.2.9)

They call us to the discovery of a realm deep within ourselves which is our native state:

> In the city of Brahman is a secret dwelling, the lotus of the heart. Within this dwelling is a space, and within that space is the fulfillment of our desires. . . .

> Never fear that old age will invade that city; never fear that this inner treasure of all reality will wither and decay. This knows no aging when the body ages; this knows no dying when the body dies.
>
> (Chandogya VIII.1.1.5)

They place us at home in a compassionate universe, where nothing is "other" than ourselves – and they urge us to treat that universe with reverence, for there is nothing in the world but God:

> The Self is the sun shining in the sky,
> The wind blowing in space; he is the fire
> At the altar and in the home the guest;
> He dwells in human beings, in gods, in truth,
> And in the vast firmament; he is the fish
> Born in water, the plant growing in the earth,
> The river flowing down from the mountain.
> For this Self is supreme!
>
> (Katha II.2.2)

What does it mean to say that nothing is separate and God alone is real? Certainly not that the everyday world is an illu-

sion. The illusion is simply that we appear separate; the underlying reality is that all of life is one. The Upanishads view the
world in grades of significance: as waking is a higher reality
than dreaming, so there is a level of reality higher than that.
All experience is real. Confusion arises only when a dream
experience is treated as reality after one awakes – or when life
is viewed as nothing but sensation, without wholeness, meaning, or goal. The ideal of the Upanishads is to live in the world
in full awareness of life's unity, giving and enjoying, participating in others' sorrows and joys, but never unaware even
for a moment that the world comes from God and returns to
God.

Last, most significantly, the Upanishads tell us that our
native state is a realm where death cannot reach, which can be
attained here in this life by those willing to devote their lives
to the necessary purification of consciousness:

> When all desires that surge in the heart
> Are renounced, the mortal becomes immortal.
> When all the knots that strangle the heart
> Are loosened, the mortal becomes immortal.
> This sums up the teaching of the scriptures.
> (Katha II.3.14–15)

We should pause to understand the significance of such
words, for nowhere do the Upanishads reach loftier heights.
In the Vedic hymns, death meant roughly what other religions
promise: transport of the soul, the "bright body," to everlast-

ing life in a heaven of bliss. The sages understood this "bright body"; they knew firsthand that when the Self withdraws consciousness from the body, the continuity of personality is not broken. Death would not be different:

> As a caterpillar, having come to the end of one blade of
> grass, draws itself together and reaches out for the next,
> so the Self, having come to the end of one life and shed all
> ignorance, gathers in its faculties and reaches out from the
> old body to a new.
>
> (Brihadaranyaka III.4.3)

But they also knew that ultimately body and mind are made of the same primal energy, called *prana*, and that everything created must someday be dissolved. If personality returns life after life, then heaven too must be only a state of consciousness, part of the created world. It might last longer and be more blissful than bodily existence, but heaven too had to be transitory: a kind of interregnum in another *loka* or "world," in which the Self can look back and learn from past mistakes.

In this compassionate view life becomes a kind of school in which the individual self is constantly evolving, growing life after life toward a fully human stature. The goal is realization of one's true nature: not matter, embodied or disembodied, but the uncreated Self:

> The world is the wheel of God, turning round
> And round with all living creatures upon its rim.
> The world is the river of God,

Flowing from him and flowing back to him.
On this ever-revolving wheel of being
The individual self goes round and round
Through life after life, believing itself
To be a separate creature, until
It sees its identity with the Lord of Love
And attains immortality in the indivisible whole.

(Shvetashvatara 1.4–6)

Thus Self-realization is immortality in an entirely new sense: not "everlasting life" but beyond death and life alike. In this state, when death comes, one sheds the body with no more rupture in consciousness than we feel in taking off a jacket at the end of the day.

In all of this, we need to remember that the Upanishads present no system. When, much later, India's mystics and philosophers did build coherent structures on these foundations, they found they had produced points of logical disagreement. But all understood that in practice such systems come to the same thing; they simply appeal in different ways to the head and heart.

No one has explained this better than Sri Ramakrishna, the towering mystic of nineteenth-century Bengal who followed each path to the same goal: these are simply views from different vantage points, not higher or lower and not in conflict. From one point of view the world is God; from another, there will always be a veil of difference between an embodied human person and the Godhead. Both are true, and neither is the whole truth. Reality is beyond all limitations, and there are paths to it to accommodate every heart.

In the end, then, the Upanishads belong not just to Hinduism. They are India's most precious legacy to humanity, and in that spirit they are offered here.

॥॰

THE UPANISHADS

॰॥

Translated by Eknath Easwaran
Chapter Introductions & Afterword
by Michael N. Nagler

▯ *Isha Upanishad*

The Self is everywhere. Bright is the Self,
Indivisible, untouched by sin, wise,
Immanent and transcendent. He it is
Who holds the cosmos together.

[8]

▮: *The Inner Ruler*

"IF ALL THE UPANISHADS AND ALL the other scriptures happened all of a sudden to be reduced to ashes, and if only the first verse in the Ishopanishad were left in the memory of the Hindus, Hinduism would live forever."

With these words Mahatma Gandhi paid tribute to the remarkable Upanishad that traditionally stands at the beginning of most Indian collections. It owes this priority to the poetic grandeur and sustained profundity of its language, which in only eighteen verses establish the fundamental building blocks of spiritual awareness.

What Gandhi had in mind with his great tribute he made clear in his reply to a journalist who wanted the secret of his life in three words: "Renounce and enjoy!" (*tena tyaktena bhuñjītāḥ*), from the first verse of the Isha.

The fifth-century Greek writer we know as Dionysius the Areopagite once said that as he grew older and wiser his books got shorter and shorter. He would have envied the sage of this Upanishad. In its intensity he does not mince words. The central section, verses 9–14, is what scholars call a "crux," or famously difficult passage. The translation brings out its practical significance: materialism leads us to lose awareness of our inner life, which is bad enough; but to be hypnotized by our own feelings and sensations and forget about others and the world around us is worse. By living in awareness of both these worlds, we can rise above them toward the one Reality. With the last four verses we emerge onto that lofty plane, and the Upanishad takes on a tone of intense devotion that is rare even in later, God-centered mystical literature.

Each Upanishad comes with an invocation drawn from a traditional set. The invocation to the Isha is especially striking. Consistent with the condensed meaning of the Upanishad itself, it rings changes on a simple household word, "full" (*purnam*): in the inexhaustible Reality, the infinite of "that" world, the unseen, sends forth "this" world of infinite variety in which we live, without ever being diminished. The American poet Anne Sexton may have been thinking of this haunting invocation when she wrote:

> Then the well spoke to me.
> It said: Abundance is scooped from abundance
> yet abundance remains.

This is a very Gandhian idea. Materialism reinforces a "paradigm of scarcity": there is not enough to go around, so we are doomed to fight one another for ever-diminishing resources. Spiritual economics begins not from the assumed scarcity of matter but from the verifiable infinitude of consciousness. "Think of this One original source," Plotinus said, "as a spring, self-generating, feeding all of itself to the rivers and yet not used up by them, ever at rest." Or, as Gandhi put it, "There is enough in the world for everyone's need; there is not enough for everyone's greed." The appearance of scarcity overcomes those for whom, as the Upanishad says, "the world without alone is real." There is no scarcity of love, respect, meaning – the resources of consciousness. Such is the timeless wisdom of the Upanishads.

– M . N .

All this is full. All that is full.
From fullness, fullness comes.
When fullness is taken from fullness,
Fullness still remains.

O M *shanti shanti shanti*

1: *The Isha Upanishad*

[1] The Lord is enshrined in the hearts of all.
The Lord is the supreme Reality.
Rejoice in him through renunciation.
Covet nothing. All belongs to the Lord.
[2] Thus working may you live a hundred years.
Thus alone will you work in real freedom.

[3] Those who deny the Self are born again
Blind to the Self, enveloped in darkness,
Utterly devoid of love for the Lord.

[4] The Self is one. Ever still, the Self is
Swifter than thought, swifter than the senses.
Though motionless, he outruns all pursuit.
Without the Self, never could life exist.

[5] The Self seems to move, but is ever still.
He seems far away, but is ever near.
He is within all, and he transcends all.

⁶ Those who see all creatures in themselves
And themselves in all creatures know no fear.
⁷ Those who see all creatures in themselves
And themselves in all creatures know no grief.
How can the multiplicity of life
Delude the one who sees its unity?

⁸ The Self is everywhere. Bright is the Self,
Indivisible, untouched by sin, wise,
Immanent and transcendent. He it is
Who holds the cosmos together.

⁹⁻¹¹ In dark night live those for whom
The world without alone is real; in night
Darker still, for whom the world within
Alone is real. The first leads to a life
Of action, the second to a life of meditation.
But those who combine action with meditation
Cross the sea of death through action
And enter into immortality
Through the practice of meditation.
So have we heard from the wise.

¹²⁻¹⁴ In dark night live those for whom the Lord
Is transcendent only; in night darker still,
For whom he is immanent only.
But those for whom he is transcendent

And immanent cross the sea of death
With the immanent and enter into
Immortality with the transcendent.
So have we heard from the wise.

¹⁵ The face of truth is hidden by your orb
Of gold, O sun. May you remove your orb
So that I, who adore the true, may see
The glory of truth. ¹⁶ O nourishing sun,
Solitary traveler, controller,
Source of life for all creatures, spread your light
And subdue your dazzling splendor
So that I may see your blessed Self.
Even that very Self am I!

¹⁷ May my life merge in the Immortal
When my body is reduced to ashes.
O mind, meditate on the eternal Brahman.
Remember the deeds of the past.
Remember, O mind, remember.

¹⁸ O god of fire, lead us by the good path
To eternal joy. You know all our deeds.
Deliver us from evil, we who bow
And pray again and again.

OM *shanti shanti shanti*

II: *The Katha Upanishad*

When a person dies, there arises this doubt:
"He still exists," say some; "he does not,"
Say others. I want you to teach me the truth.

[1.1.20]

▯: *Death as Teacher*

IF THERE IS ONE UPANISHAD THAT can be called a favorite in all ages, it is the Katha. It is not hard to see why. Its theme, broadly, is the same as that of all the Upanishads: the deathless Self, the need for and the way to its realization; but the Katha is more successful than other Upanishads at describing this, in several ways.

As the Upanishads illustrate, the right questions are half the battle in life. In the Katha we have the right question in highly dramatic form; in fact we have a highly imaginative confrontation of the ideal teacher (1.1.22) and the ideal student (11.1.4), and their identity is surprising: the latter is a teenager, and his teacher is death.

We must consider why.

Nothing places the question "Who am I?" in such stark relief as the fact of death. What dies? What is left? Are we here merely to be torn away from everyone, and everyone from us? And what, if anything, can we do about death – now, while we are still alive?

Most social life seems a conspiracy to discourage us from thinking of these questions. But there is a rare type for whom death is present every moment, putting his grim question mark to every aspect of life, and that person cannot rest without some answers. It can happen to anyone: in the "fall of a sparrow," a dead animal on the freeway, news reports of some faraway natural disaster, the passing of an old friend, or a new one; in some chance reminder of the violence that is not far from any of us, in all these that unwelcome Presence can make itself briefly but urgently known.

Nachiketa represents that rare type of awakened person in whom this presence, once glimpsed, can never go away. "Now that I have seen your face," he says to Death, "what can I enjoy?" Yet, rare as he is, he represents the capacity latent in all of us to face that grim awareness and use it as a drive to deepening consciousness.

In other Upanishads and throughout Indian literature allegory is a favorite device, but rarely is it more dynamic and successful than in the Katha. The opening narrative is an extended allegory which keeps spiritual depth and dramatic vividness in high suspense: the story never becomes unreal and its archetypal significance never becomes invisible; neither is mere vehicle or signifier for the other. Every detail has both immediate and transcendent reality (in some cases making translation unusually inadequate). Nachiketa, who has more personality than most Upanishadic figures, asks, as an abstraction could not, "What is death going to do with me, today?" But at the same time he immediately universalizes his condition, which is in fact the most universal of human destinies: "I shall go to death, at the head of many more to follow. . . ." That Nachiketa is consigned to death by his own father cries out for allegorical interpretation, and it is not hard to supply. As Julian of Norwich, a fourteenth-century English anchoress and mystic, wrote, "We wot that our parents do but bear us into death. A strange thing, that." Birth is but the beginning of a trajectory to death; for all their love, parents cannot halt it and in a sense have "given us to death" merely by giving us birth.

As for the student, we can only pause in admiration of this ancient civilization whose hero is a teenager who has not learned the rudimentary grace of civilized existence – to hold his peace in the presence of hypocrisy. Nachiketa is an attractive character who cannot go along with sham; but he is not an obstreperous rebel: he is more sincere about convention than his father (including the convention of obedience to a father even when the latter has lost his temper) and his first wish is for reconciliation with him. At no time does he lack respect. But that is just the point; he forces the issue by taking the demands of religion seriously when the majority have long since allowed external observance to paper it over, making of it a dead letter that no longer communicates anything about personal struggle. But by poking holes in society's shroud of complacency he represents, again, what it would take to awaken any and all of us. The text sums it up in the single trait it tells us about the lad. He has *shraddha*: determined seriousness, a deep, abiding, confident faith.

In structure and content, the Katha is more of an organic whole than any but the briefest Upanishads. It begins with a prose narrative of the "once upon a time" variety, sounding very much like its source story in the Brahmanas, but it quickly enters a gripping dramatic situation with the characters' speeches in verse.

Then follows the encounter of Nachiketa with Death, and its dramatic reversal when he passes Death's severe test and changes him from gruff and off-putting deity to delighted teacher. Though this interpersonal drama falls into the background during the subsequent teaching, it comes back as it were triumphantly at the end of the Upanishad, along with several key words and the major themes of the question for which Nachiketa had gone to the king of death to find some answer.

The Katha consistently lays stress on several practical themes of the spiritual life: that a spiritual teacher is essential; that in all human experience it is really only the Self, pure consciousness, that is the enjoyer, so that when one realizes the Self "there is nothing else to be known" and "all the knots that strangle the heart are loosened"; and of course that death occurs only to that part of us which was born and launched into separate existence. This Upanishad thus speaks to a longing which could not be deeper or more universal: that some day, somehow, as Donne put it, "Death shall be no more: Death, thou shalt die!"

The Katha is also distinctive in explaining with the use of two very practical terms that every moment we live, even theoretically while we sleep, we face a steep choice between what will move us closer to that day and what will only postpone it – that is, between what is good and what is merely pleasant; in Sanskrit, between *shreya* and *preya*. While there are no dualities and no compartments in reality, as long as there are dualities and compartments in personality, we have to pay careful attention to this distinction at every moment. But that makes life very much worth living; and perhaps in this sense, as Wallace Stevens wrote in "Sunday Morning":

> Death is the mother of beauty; hence from her,
> Alone, shall come fulfillment to our dreams
> And our desires.

– M . N .

May the Lord of Love protect us.
May the Lord of Love nourish us.
May the Lord of Love strengthen us.
May we realize the Lord of Love.
May we live with love for all;
May we live in peace with all.

O M *shanti shanti shanti*

II: *The Katha Upanishad*

PART I

[1]

¹ Once, long ago, Vajasravasa gave away his possessions to gain religious merit. He had a son named Nachiketa who, ² though only a boy, was full of faith in the scriptures. Nachiketa thought when the offerings were made: ³ "What merit can one obtain by giving away cows that are too old to give milk?"

⁴ To help his father understand this, Nachiketa said: "To whom will you offer me?" He asked this again and again. "To death I give you!" said his father in anger.

⁵ The son thought: "I go, the first of many who will die, in the midst of many who are dying, on a mission to Yama, king of death.

⁶ See how it was with those who came before,
How it will be with those who are living.

Like corn mortals ripen and fall; like corn
They come up again."

Nachiketa went to Yama's abode, but the king of death
was not there. He waited three days. When Yama
returned, he heard a voice say:

⁷ "When a spiritual guest enters the house,
Like a bright flame, he must be received well,
With water to wash his feet. ⁸ Far from wise
Are those who are not hospitable
To such a guest. They will lose all their hopes,
The religious merit they have acquired,
Their sons and their cattle."

YAMA

⁹ O spiritual guest, I grant you three boons
To atone for the three inhospitable nights
You have spent in my abode.
Ask for three boons, one for each night.

NACHIKETA

¹⁰ O king of death, as the first of these boons
Grant that my father's anger be appeased,
So he may recognize me when I return
And receive me with love.

YAMA

[11] I grant that your father, the son of Uddalaka
  and Aruna,
Will love you as in the past. When he sees you
Released from the jaws of death, he will sleep
Again with a mind at peace.

NACHIKETA

[12] There is no fear at all in heaven; for you
Are not there, neither old age nor death.
Passing beyond hunger and thirst and pain,
All rejoice in the kingdom of heaven.

[13] You know the fire sacrifice that leads to heaven,
O king of death. I have full faith
In you and ask for instruction. Let this
Be your second boon to me.

YAMA

[14] Yes, I do know, Nachiketa, and shall
Teach you the fire sacrifice that leads
To heaven and sustains the world, that knowledge
Concealed in the heart. Now listen.

THE NARRATOR

[15] Then the king of death taught Nachiketa how to
perform the fire sacrifice, how to erect the altar for
worshipping the fire from which the universe evolves.

When the boy repeated his instruction, the dread king
of death was well pleased and said:

YAMA

[16] Let me give you a special boon: this sacrifice
Shall be called by your name, Nachiketa.
Accept from me this many-hued chain too.
[17] Those who have thrice performed this sacrifice,
Realized their unity with father, mother,
And teacher, and discharged the three duties
Of studying the scriptures, ritual worship,
And giving alms to those in need, rise above
Birth and death. Knowing the god of fire
Born of Brahman, they attain perfect peace.
[18] Those who carry out this triple duty
Conscious of its full meaning will shake off
The dread noose of death and transcend sorrow
To enjoy the world of heaven.

[19] Thus have I granted you the second boon,
Nachiketa, the secret of the fire
That leads to heaven. It will have your name.
Ask now, Nachiketa, for the third boon.

NACHIKETA

[20] When a person dies, there arises this doubt:
"He still exists," say some; "he does not,"

Say others. I want you to teach me the truth.
This is my third boon.

YAMA

[21] This doubt haunted even the gods of old,
For the secret of death is hard to know.
Nachiketa, ask for some other boon
And release me from my promise.

NACHIKETA

[22] This doubt haunted even the gods of old;
For it is hard to know, O Death, as you say.
I can have no greater teacher than you,
And there is no boon equal to this.

YAMA

[23] Ask for sons and grandsons who will live
A hundred years. Ask for herds of cattle,
Elephants and horses, gold and vast land,
And ask to live as long as you desire.
[24] Or, if you can think of anything more
Desirable, ask for that, with wealth and
Long life as well. Nachiketa, be the ruler
Of a great kingdom, and I will give you
The utmost capacity to enjoy
The pleasures of life. [25] Ask for beautiful
Women of loveliness rarely seen on earth,

Riding in chariots, skilled in music,
To attend on you. But Nachiketa,
Don't ask me about the secret of death.

NACHIKETA

26 These pleasures last but until tomorrow,
And they wear out the vital powers of life.
How fleeting is all life on earth! Therefore
Keep your horses and chariots, dancing
And music, for yourself. 27 Never can mortals
Be made happy by wealth. How can we be
Desirous of wealth when we see your face
And know we cannot live while you are here?
This is the boon I choose and ask you for.

28 Having approached an immortal like you,
How can I, subject to old age and death,
Ever try to rejoice in a long life
For the sake of the senses' fleeting pleasures?
29 Dispel this doubt of mine, O king of death:
Does a person live after death or does he not?
Nachiketa asks for no other boon
Than the secret of this great mystery.

[2]

YAMA

¹ The joy of the spirit ever abides,
But not what seems pleasant to the senses.
Both these, differing in their purpose, prompt
Us to action. All is well for those who choose
The joy of the spirit, but they miss
The goal of life who prefer the pleasant.
² Perennial joy or passing pleasure?
This is the choice one is to make always.
Those who are wise recognize this, but not
The ignorant. The first welcome what leads
To abiding joy, though painful at the time.
The latter run, goaded by their senses,
After what seems immediate pleasure.
³ Well have you renounced these passing pleasures
So dear to the senses, Nachiketa,
And turned your back on the way of the world
That makes mankind forget the goal of life.

⁴ Far apart are wisdom and ignorance.
The first leads one to Self-realization;
The second makes one more and more
Estranged from one's real Self. I regard you,
Nachiketa, as worthy of instruction,
For passing pleasures tempt you not at all.

5 Ignorant of their ignorance, yet wise
In their own esteem, those deluded men
Proud of their vain learning go round and round
Like the blind led by the blind. 6 Far beyond
Their eyes, hypnotized by the world of sense,
Opens the way to immortality.
"I am my body; when my body dies,
I die." Living in this superstition,
They fall life after life under my sway.

7 It is but few who hear about the Self.
Fewer still dedicate their lives to its
Realization. Wonderful is the one
Who speaks about the Self. Rare are they
Who make it the supreme goal of their lives.
Blessed are they who, through an illumined
Teacher, attain to Self-realization.

8 The truth of the Self cannot come through one
Who has not realized that he is the Self.
The intellect cannot reveal the Self,
Beyond its duality of subject
And object. Those who see themselves in all
And all in them help others through spiritual
Osmosis to realize the Self themselves.
9 This awakening you have known comes not
Through logic and scholarship, but from

Close association with a realized teacher.
Wise are you, Nachiketa, because you
Seek the Self eternal. May we have more
Seekers like you!

NACHIKETA

¹⁰ I know that earthly treasures are transient,
And never can I reach the eternal through them.
Hence have I renounced all my desires for earthly
    treasures
To win the eternal through your instruction.

YAMA

¹¹ I spread before your eyes, Nachiketa,
The fulfillment of all worldly desires:
Power to dominate the earth, delights
Celestial gained through religious rites,
Miraculous powers beyond time and space.
These with will and wisdom have you renounced.

¹² The wise, realizing through meditation
The timeless Self, beyond all perception,
Hidden in the cave of the heart,
Leave pain and pleasure far behind.
¹³ Those who know they are neither body nor mind
But the immemorial Self, the divine
Principle of existence, find the source

Of all joy and live in joy abiding.
I see the gates of joy are opening
For you, Nachiketa.

NACHIKETA

¹⁴ Teach me of That you see as beyond right
And wrong, cause and effect, past and future.

YAMA

¹⁵ I will give you the Word all the scriptures
Glorify, all spiritual disciplines
Express, to attain which aspirants lead
A life of sense-restraint and self-naughting.
¹⁶ It is OM. This symbol of the Godhead
Is the highest. Realizing it one finds
Complete fulfillment of all one's longings.
¹⁷ It is of the greatest support to all seekers.
When OM reverberates unceasingly
Within the heart, that one is indeed blessed
And deeply loved as one who is the Self.

¹⁸ The all-knowing Self was never born,
Nor will it die. Beyond cause and effect,
This Self is eternal and immutable.
When the body dies, the Self does not die.
¹⁹ If the slayer believes that he can kill
Or the slain believes that he can be killed,

Neither knows the truth. The eternal Self
Slays not, nor is ever slain.

20 Hidden in the heart of every creature
Exists the Self, subtler than the subtlest,
Greater than the greatest. They go beyond
All sorrow who extinguish their self-will
And behold the glory of the Self
Through the grace of the Lord of Love.

21 Though one sits in meditation in a
Particular place, the Self within
Can exercise his influence far away.
Though still, he moves everything everywhere.

22 When the wise realize the Self,
Formless in the midst of forms, changeless
In the midst of change, omnipresent
And supreme, they go beyond sorrow.

23 The Self cannot be known through study
Of the scriptures, nor through the intellect,
Nor through hearing discourses about it.
The Self can be attained only by those
Whom the Self chooses. Verily unto them
Does the Self reveal himself.

²⁴ The Self cannot be known by anyone
Who desists not from unrighteous ways,
Controls not the senses, stills not the mind,
And practices not meditation.

²⁵ None else can know the omnipresent Self,
Whose glory sweeps away the rituals
Of the priest and the prowess of the warrior
And puts death itself to death.

[3]

¹ In the secret cave of the heart, two are
Seated by life's fountain. The separate ego
Drinks of the sweet and bitter stuff,
Liking the sweet, disliking the bitter,
While the supreme Self drinks sweet and bitter
Neither liking this nor disliking that.
The ego gropes in darkness, while the Self
Lives in light. So declare the illumined sages
And the householders who worship
The sacred fire in the name of the Lord.

² May we light the fire of Nachiketa
That burns out the ego and enables us
To pass from fearful fragmentation
To fearless fullness in the changeless whole.

3 Know the Self as lord of the chariot,

The body as the chariot itself,

The discriminating intellect as

The charioteer, and the mind as reins.

4 The senses, say the wise, are the horses;

Selfish desires are the roads they travel.

When the Self is confused with the body,

Mind, and senses, they point out, he seems

To enjoy pleasure and suffer sorrow.

5 When a person lacks discrimination

And his mind is undisciplined, the senses

Run hither and thither like wild horses.

6 But they obey the rein like trained horses

When one has discrimination and

Has made the mind one-pointed. 7 Those who lack

Discrimination, with little control

Over their thoughts and far from pure,

Reach not the pure state of immortality

But wander from death to death; 8 but those

Who have discrimination, with a still mind

And a pure heart, reach journey's end,

Never again to fall into the jaws of death.

9 With a discriminating intellect

As charioteer and a trained mind as reins,

They attain the supreme goal of life,
To be united with the Lord of Love.

¹⁰ The senses derive from objects of sense-perception,
Sense objects from mind, mind from intellect,
And intellect from ego; ¹¹ ego from undifferentiated
Consciousness, and consciousness from Brahman.
Brahman is the First Cause and last refuge.
¹² Brahman, the hidden Self in everyone,
Does not shine forth. He is revealed only
To those who keep their minds one-pointed
On the Lord of Love and thus develop
A superconscious manner of knowing.
¹³ Meditation enables them to go
Deeper and deeper into consciousness,
From the world of words to the world of thoughts,
Then beyond thoughts to wisdom in the Self.

¹⁴ Get up! Wake up! Seek the guidance of an
Illumined teacher and realize the Self.
Sharp like a razor's edge, the sages say,
Is the path, difficult to traverse.

¹⁵ The supreme Self is beyond name and form,
Beyond the senses, inexhaustible,
Without beginning, without end, beyond
Time, space, and causality, eternal,

Immutable. Those who realize the Self
Are forever free from the jaws of death.

[16] The wise, who gain experiential knowledge
Of this timeless tale of Nachiketa,
Narrated by Death, attain the glory
Of living in spiritual awareness.
Those who, full of devotion, recite this
Supreme mystery at a spiritual
Gathering are fit for eternal life.
They are indeed fit for eternal life.

PART II

[1]

[1] The self-existent Lord pierced the senses
To turn outward. Thus we look to the world
Without and see not the Self within us.
A sage withdrew his senses from the world
Of change and, seeking immortality,
Looked within and beheld the deathless Self.

[2] The immature run after sense pleasures
And fall into the widespread net of death.
But the wise, knowing the Self as deathless,
Seek not the changeless in the world of change.

³ That through which one enjoys form, taste,
      smell, sound,
Touch, and sexual union is the Self.
Can there be anything not known to That
Who is the One in all? Know One, know all.
⁴ That through which one enjoys the waking
And sleeping states is the Self. To know That
As consciousness is to go beyond sorrow.
⁵ Those who know the Self as enjoyer
Of the honey from the flowers of the senses,
Ever present within, ruler of time,
Go beyond fear. For this Self is supreme!

⁶ The god of creation, Brahma,
Born of the Godhead through meditation
Before the waters of life were created,
Who stands in the heart of every creature,
Is the Self indeed. For this Self is supreme!

⁷ The goddess of energy, Aditi,
Born of the Godhead through vitality,
Mother of all the cosmic forces,
Who stands in the heart of every creature,
Is the Self indeed. For this Self is supreme!

⁸ The god of fire, Agni, hidden between
Two firesticks like a child well protected

In the mother's womb, whom we adore
Every day in the depths of meditation,
Is the Self indeed. For this Self is supreme!

9 That which is the source of the sun
And of every power in the cosmos, beyond which
There is neither going nor coming,
Is the Self indeed. For this Self is supreme!

10 What is here is also there; what is there,
Also here. Who sees multiplicity
But not the one indivisible Self
Must wander on and on from death to death.

11 Only the one-pointed mind attains
This state of unity. There is no one
But the Self. Who sees multiplicity
But not the one indivisible Self
Must wander on and on from death to death.

12 That thumb-sized being enshrined in the heart,
Ruler of time, past and future,
To see whom is to go beyond all fear,
Is the Self indeed. For this Self is supreme!

13 That thumb-sized being, a flame without smoke,
Ruler of time, past and future,

The same on this day as on tomorrow,
Is the Self indeed. For this Self is supreme!

[14] As the rain on a mountain peak runs off
The slopes on all sides, so those who see
Only the seeming multiplicity of life
Run after things on every side.

[15] As pure water poured into pure water
Becomes the very same, so does the Self
Of the illumined man or woman, Nachiketa,
Verily become one with the Godhead.

[2]

[1] There is a city with eleven gates
Of which the ruler is the unborn Self,
Whose light forever shines. They go beyond
Sorrow who meditate on the Self and
Are freed from the cycle of birth and death.
For this Self is supreme!

[2] The Self is the sun shining in the sky,
The wind blowing in space; he is the fire
At the altar and in the home the guest;
He dwells in human beings, in gods, in truth,
And in the vast firmament; he is the fish
Born in water, the plant growing in the earth,

The river flowing down from the mountain.
For this Self is supreme!

³ The adorable one who is seated
In the heart rules the breath of life.
Unto him all the senses pay their homage.
⁴ When the dweller in the body breaks out
In freedom from the bonds of flesh,
What remains? For this Self is supreme!

⁵ We live not by the breath that flows in
And flows out, but by him who causes the breath
To flow in and flow out.

⁶ Now, O Nachiketa, I will tell you
Of this unseen, eternal Brahman, and
What befalls the Self after death. ⁷ Of those
Unaware of the Self, some are born as
Embodied creatures while others remain
In a lower stage of evolution,
As determined by their own need for growth.

⁸ That which is awake even in our sleep,
Giving form in dreams to the objects of
Sense craving, that indeed is pure light,
Brahman the immortal, who contains all
The cosmos, and beyond whom none can go.
For this Self is supreme!

⁹ As the same fire assumes different shapes
When it consumes objects differing in shape,
So does the one Self take the shape
Of every creature in whom he is present.
¹⁰ As the same air assumes different shapes
When it enters objects differing in shape,
So does the one Self take the shape
Of every creature in whom he is present.

¹¹ As the sun, who is the eye of the world,
Cannot be tainted by the defects in our eyes
Or by the objects it looks on,
So the one Self, dwelling in all, cannot
Be tainted by the evils of the world.
For this Self transcends all!

¹² The ruler supreme, inner Self of all,
Multiplies his oneness into many.
Eternal joy is theirs who see the Self
In their own hearts. To none else does it come!

¹³ Changeless amidst the things that pass away,
Pure consciousness in all who are conscious,
The One answers the prayers of many.
Eternal peace is theirs who see the Self
In their own hearts. To none else does it come!

NACHIKETA

14 How can I know that blissful Self, supreme,
Inexpressible, realized by the wise?
Is he the light, or does he reflect light?

YAMA

15 There shines not the sun, neither moon nor star,
Nor flash of lightning, nor fire lit on earth.
The Self is the light reflected by all.
He shining, everything shines after him.

[3]

1 The Tree of Eternity has its roots above
And its branches on earth below.
Its pure root is Brahman the immortal,
From whom all the worlds draw their life, and whom
None can transcend. For this Self is supreme!

2 The cosmos comes forth from Brahman and moves
In him. With his power it reverberates,
Like thunder crashing in the sky. Those who
Realize him pass beyond the sway of death.

3 In fear of him fire burns; in fear of him
The sun shines, the clouds rain, and the winds blow.
In fear of him death stalks about to kill.

⁴ If one fails to realize Brahman in this life
Before the physical sheath is shed,
He must again put on a body
In the world of embodied creatures.

⁵ Brahman can be seen, as in a mirror,
In a pure heart; in the world of the ancestors
As in a dream; in the gandharva world
As the reflections in trembling waters;
And clear as light in the realm of Brahma.

⁶ Knowing the senses to be separate
From the Self, and the sense experience
To be fleeting, the wise grieve no more.

⁷ Above the senses is the mind, above
The mind is the intellect, above that
Is the ego, and above the ego
Is the unmanifested Cause.
⁸ And beyond is Brahman, omnipresent,
Attributeless. Realizing him one is released
From the cycle of birth and death.

⁹ He is formless, and can never be seen
With these two eyes. But he reveals himself
In the heart made pure through meditation
And sense-restraint. Realizing him, one is
Released from the cycle of birth and death.

¹⁰ When the five senses are stilled, when the mind
Is stilled, when the intellect is stilled,
That is called the highest state by the wise.
¹¹ They say yoga is this complete stillness
In which one enters the unitive state,
Never to become separate again.
If one is not established in this state,
The sense of unity will come and go.

¹² The unitive state cannot be attained
Through words or thoughts or through the eye.
How can it be attained except through one
Who is established in this state oneself?

¹³ There are two selves, the separate ego
And the indivisible Atman. When
One rises above *I* and *me* and *mine*,
The Atman is revealed as one's real Self.

¹⁴ When all desires that surge in the heart
Are renounced, the mortal becomes immortal.
¹⁵ When all the knots that strangle the heart
Are loosened, the mortal becomes immortal.
This sums up the teaching of the scriptures.

¹⁶ From the heart there radiate a hundred
And one vital tracks. One of them rises

To the crown of the head. This way leads
To immortality, the others to death.

[17] The Lord of Love, not larger than the thumb,
Is ever enshrined in the hearts of all.
Draw him clear out of the physical sheath,
As one draws the stalk from the *munja* grass.
Know thyself to be pure and immortal!
Know thyself to be pure and immortal!

THE NARRATOR

Nachiketa learned from the king of death
The whole discipline of meditation.
Freeing himself from all separateness,
He won immortality in Brahman.
So blessed is everyone who knows the Self!

OM *shanti shanti shanti*

▯⋮ The Brihadaranyaka Upanishad

As a caterpillar, having come to the end of one blade of grass, draws itself together and reaches out for the next, so the Self, having come to the end of one life and dispelled all ignorance, gathers in his faculties and reaches out from the old body to a new.

[IV.4.3]

❶: *The Forest of Wisdom*

BRIHAD-ARANYAKA MEANS "OF THE great forest," and that is an apt name for this Upanishad, which is by far the longest and one of the most revered of these magnificent documents. To read it is like walking through a great forest with paths leading off in unpredictable but somehow meaningful directions; we keep coming across gems of wisdom.

The opening selection illustrates this, being one of the most poignant and illuminating discussions in the wisdom of any tradition. It is the dialogue between a great sage, Yajnavalkya, and his wife Maitreyi. Yajnavalkya has just reached a critical juncture in his life: he is about to leave home in the pursuit of truth, or Self-realization. Maitreyi shares his yearning for immortality, and so the parting dialogue between them turns into a deep session of "spiritual instruction" – one of the meanings of the word *upanishad*.

What Yajnavalkya wants to teach is the greatest discovery of the Upanishads: the Self, which is identical in all of us, the

Life of all that lives. Whenever we love, he tells his wife, we are really responding to the Self within that person. There-fore – and this is the underlying theme of all mysticism – if we discover this Self in our own consciousness, there will be no more parting, no more sorrow ever. Shankara once declared that two words from the Upanishads give us the essence of all their teachings: "meditate on the Self," that is, become one with – realize – this underlying Reality.

Often, it is this anguish of parting – the death of a loved one, the breaking apart of a deep relationship, even the grow-ing up of our children – that propels us into the search for a reality that will never let us down; so this opening passage illustrates, through the experience of Maitreyi, the state of seriousness, of being shocked into alertness, that makes one ready to absorb spiritual insight. The only real source of such insight is almost always, in Indian tradition, a living teacher who is equally ready to impart it; that is why almost all the Upanishads are in the form of dialogues.

In the next two sections we again meet Yajnavalkya, now playing the important role of spiritual adviser to a famous king, Janaka, who himself was destined to achieve illumina-tion. Illustrating the wry humor of the Upanishads and the very human way they see even the most august sages at III.7 Yajnavalkya perks up on hearing that King Janaka will give a thousand cows to the wisest among the gathered pundits and casually tells his disciple, "Son, drive them home." Then,

when the outraged brahmins ask how he dares declare himself the wisest among them, he disarms them by saying, "I
bow down to the wisest, but I want those cows!" Challenged
by Gargi, another of those women of spiritual authority who
appear in the Upanishads, the sage explains how all existence – everything in the phenomenal world – is "woven" in
the Imperishable. To bring across this great truth he relies on
wonderfully vivid images. The human being moves between
two main states of consciousness as a great fish, master of its
world, swims back and forth between the banks of a river; like
a tired eagle returning to its nest at last, we find our true home
in the eternal Self, the source of all awareness. Or, boldly, "as
one in the arms of his beloved is not aware of what is without
or what is within, so one in union with the Self is not aware of
what is without or what is within," for all desires are fulfilled.

When we encounter this daring vision of reality, we want to
know what to *do.* If this tremendous vision is to have any ultimate meaning for us, there must be some way we can at least
partly realize it ourselves. Appropriately, then, this selection
ends with a passage that, while lightly disguised as mythology, highlights three potent practices: *dāmyata datta dayadhvam,* "Be self-controlled, give, be compassionate." This passage, boiled down as it is to three potent syllables, *da – da –
da*, caught the imagination of T. S. Eliot; more to the point,
it has helped countless seekers down the ages to orient their
lives to the supreme goal.   – M . N .

All this is full. All that is full.
From fullness, fullness comes.
When fullness is taken from fullness,
Fullness still remains.

O M *shanti shanti shanti*

0: *The Brihadaranyaka Upanishad*

CHAPTER II

The Path to Immortality

4.1 "Maitreyi," Yajnavalkya said to his wife one day, "the time has come for me to go forth from the worldly life. Come, my dear, let me divide my property between you and Katyayani."

MAITREYI

4.2 My lord, if I could get all the wealth in the world, would it help me to go beyond death?

YAJNAVALKYA

Not at all. You would live and die like any other rich person. No one can buy immortality with money.

MAITREYI

4.3 Of what use then are money and material possessions to me? Please tell me, my lord, of the way that leads to immortality.

YAJNAVALKYA

4.4 You have always been dear to me, Maitreyi, and I love you even more now that you have asked me about immortality. Sit here by my side and reflect deeply on what I say.

4.5 A wife loves her husband not for his own sake, dear, but because the Self lives in him.

A husband loves his wife not for her own sake, dear, but because the Self lives in her.

Children are loved not for their own sake, but because the Self lives in them.

Wealth is loved not for its own sake, but because the Self lives in it.

Brahmins are loved not for their own sake, but because the Self lives in them.

Kshatriyas are loved not for their own sake, but because the Self lives in them.

The universe is loved not for its own sake, but because the Self lives in it.

The gods are loved not for their own sake, but because the Self lives in them.

Creatures are loved not for their own sake, but because the Self lives in them.

Everything is loved not for its own sake, but because the Self lives in it.

This Self has to be realized. Hear about this Self and meditate upon him, Maitreyi. When you hear about the Self, meditate upon the Self, and finally realize the Self, you come to understand everything in life.

4.6 For brahmins confuse those who regard them as separate from the Self. Kshatriyas confuse those who regard them as separate from the Self. The universe confuses those who regard it as separate from the Self. Gods and creatures confuse those who regard them as separate from the Self. Everything confuses those who regard things as separate from the Self.

Brahmins, kshatriyas, creatures, the universe, the gods, everything: these are the Self.

4.7 No one can understand the sounds of a drum without understanding both drum and drummer; 4.8 nor the sounds of a conch without understanding both the conch and its blower; 4.9 nor the sounds of a vina without understanding both vina and musician. 4.10 As clouds of smoke arise from a fire laid with damp fuel, even so from the Supreme have issued forth all the Vedas, history, arts, sciences, poetry, aphorisms, and commentaries. All these are the breath of the Supreme.

4.11 As there can be no water without the sea, no touch without the skin, no smell without the nose, no taste without the tongue, no form without the eye, no sound without the ear, no thought without the mind, no wisdom without the heart, no work without hands, no walking without feet, no scriptures without the word, so there can be nothing without the Self.

4.12 As a lump of salt thrown in water dissolves and cannot be taken out again, though wherever we taste the water it is salty, even so, beloved, the separate self dissolves in the sea of pure consciousness, infinite and immortal. Separateness arises from identifying the Self with the body, which is made up of the elements; when this physical identification dissolves, there can be no more separate self. This is what I want to tell you, beloved.

MAITREYI

4.13 I am bewildered, Blessed One, when you say there is then no separate self.

YAJNAVALKYA

Reflect on what I have said, beloved, and you will not be confused.

4.14 As long as there is separateness, one sees another as separate from oneself, hears another as separate from oneself, smells another as separate from oneself, speaks to another as separate from oneself, thinks of another as separate from oneself, knows another as separate from oneself. But when the Self is realized as the indivisible unity of life, who can be seen by whom, who can be heard by whom, who can be smelled by whom, who can be spoken to by whom, who can be thought of by whom, who can be known by whom? Maitreyi, my beloved, how can the knower ever be known?

CHAPTER III

The Imperishable

[I]

1 King Janaka of Videha once performed a lavish sacrifice and distributed many gifts. Many wise men from Kuru and Panchala attended the ceremony, and Janaka wanted to know who was the wisest among them. So he drove a thousand cows into a pen, and between the horns of each cow he fastened ten gold

coins. [2] Then he said: "Venerable brahmins, these cows are for the wisest one among you. Let him take them away."

None of the other brahmins dared to speak, but Yajnavalkya said to his pupil Samashrava: "Son, you can drive these cows home." "Hero of seers!" his pupil exclaimed joyfully, and he drove them home.

The other brahmins were furious. "How presumptuous!" they shouted. And Ashvala, the royal priest, asked: "Yajnavalkya, do you really believe you are the wisest of those assembled here?"

Yajnavalkya replied: "I salute the wisest, but I want those cows."

[8]

[1] Then Gargi, daughter of Vachaknu, said: "Venerable brahmins, I shall ask Yajnavalkya only two questions. If he answers them well, no one here can defeat him in a spiritual debate."

"Ask, Gargi," the sage replied.

GARGI

[2] Yajnavalkya, as a warrior from Kashi or Videha rises with bow and arrow to fell his opponent, I rise to fell you with two questions.

YAJNAVALKYA

Ask them, Gargi.

GARGI

3 That which is above heaven and below the earth, which is also between heaven and earth, which is the same through past, present, and future, in what is that woven, warp and woof? Tell me, Yajnavalkya.

YAJNAVALKYA

4 That which is above heaven and below earth, which is also between heaven and earth, which is the same through the past, present, and future – that is woven, warp and woof, in space.

GARGI

5 My first question is answered well. Now for my second question.

YAJNAVALKYA

Ask, Gargi.

GARGI

6 In what is space itself woven, warp and woof? Tell me, Yajnavalkya.

YAJNAVALKYA

7-8 The sages call it Akshara, the Imperishable. It is neither big nor small, neither long nor short, neither hot nor cold, neither bright nor dark, neither air nor space. It is without attachment, without taste, smell, or touch, without eyes, ears, tongue, mouth, breath, or mind, without movement, without limitation, without inside or outside. It consumes nothing, and nothing consumes it.

9 In perfect accord with the will of the Imperishable, sun and moon make their orbits; heaven and earth remain in place; moments, hours, days, nights, fortnights, months, and seasons become years; rivers starting from the snow-clad mountains flow east and west, north and south, to the sea.

10 Without knowing the Imperishable, Gargi, whoever performs rites and ceremonies and undergoes austerities, even for many years, reaps little benefit, because rites, ceremonies, and austerities are all perishable. Whosoever dies without knowing the Imperishable dies in a pitiable state; but those who know the Imperishable attain immortality when the body is shed at death.

11 The Imperishable is the seer, Gargi, though unseen; the hearer, though unheard; the thinker, though unthought; the knower, though unknown. Nothing other than the Imperishable can see, hear, think, or

know. It is in the Imperishable that space is woven, warp and woof.

GARGI

[12] Venerable brahmins, count yourselves fortunate if you get away with merely paying this man homage. No one can defeat Yajnavalkya in debate about Brahman.

With these words Gargi ended her questions.

CHAPTER IV

The States of Consciousness

[1] Yajnavalkya came to Janaka, king of Videha, saying to himself, "I will not talk today." But earlier, while they were discussing the fire ceremony, Yajnavalkya had promised him any boon he wanted. Now the king asked the sage permission to question him.

JANAKA

[2] Yajnavalkya, what is the light of man?

YAJNAVALKYA

The sun is our light, for by that light we sit, work, go out, and come back.

JANAKA

[3] When the sun sets, what is the light of man?

YAJNAVALKYA

The moon is our light, for by that light we sit, work, go out, and come back.

JANAKA

4 When the sun sets, Yajnavalkya, and the moon sets, what is the light of man?

YAJNAVALKYA

Fire is our light, for by that we sit, work, go out, and come back.

JANAKA

5 When the sun sets, Yajnavalkya, and the moon sets, and the fire goes out, what is the light of man?

YAJNAVALKYA

Then speech is our light, for by that we sit, work, go out, and come back. Even though we cannot see our own hand in the dark, we can hear what is said and move toward the person speaking.

JANAKA

6 When the sun sets, Yajnavalkya, and the moon sets, and the fire goes out and no one speaks, what is the light of man?

YAJNAVALKYA

The Self indeed is the light of man, your majesty, for by that we sit, work, go out, and come back.

JANAKA

7 Who is that Self?

YAJNAVALKYA

The Self, pure awareness, shines as the light within the heart, surrounded by the senses. Only seeming to think, seeming to move, the Self neither sleeps nor wakes nor dreams.

8 When the Self takes on a body, he seems to assume the body's frailties and limitations; but when he sheds the body at the time of death, the Self leaves all these behind.

9 The human being has two states of consciousness: one in this world, the other in the next. But there is a third state between them, not unlike the world of dreams, in which we are aware of both worlds, with their sorrows and joys. When a person dies, it is only the physical body that dies; that person lives on in a nonphysical body, which carries the impressions of his past life. It is these impressions that determine his next life. In this intermediate state he makes and dissolves impressions by the light of the Self.

10 In that third state of consciousness there are no chariots, no horses drawing them or roads on which to travel, but he makes up his own chariots, horses, and roads. In that state there are no joys or pleasures, but he makes up his own joys and pleasures. In that state there are no lotus ponds, no lakes, no rivers, but he makes up his own lotus ponds, lakes, and rivers. It is he who makes up all these from the impressions of his past or waking life.

11-13 It is said of these states of consciousness that in the dreaming state, when one is sleeping, the shining Self, who never dreams, who is ever awake, watches by his own light the dreams woven out of past deeds and present desires. In the dreaming state, when one is sleeping, the shining Self keeps the body alive with the vital force of prana, and wanders wherever he wills. In the dreaming state, when one is sleeping, the shining Self assumes many forms, eats with friends, indulges in sex, sees fearsome spectacles.

16-17 But he is not affected by anything because he is detached and free; and after wandering here and there in the state of dreaming, enjoying pleasures and seeing good and evil, he returns to the state from which he began.

[18] As a great fish swims between the banks of a river as it likes, so does the shining Self move between the states of dreaming and waking.

[19] As an eagle, weary after soaring in the sky, folds its wings and flies down to rest in its nest, so does the shining Self enter the state of dreamless sleep, where one is freed from all desires.

[21] The Self is free from desire, free from evil, free from fear.

As a man in the arms of his beloved is not aware of what is without and what is within, so a person in union with the Self is not aware of what is without and what is within, for in that unitive state all desires find their perfect fulfillment. There is no other desire that needs to be fulfilled, and one goes beyond sorrow.

[22] In that unitive state there is neither father nor mother, neither worlds nor gods nor even scriptures. In that state there is neither thief nor slayer, neither low caste nor high, neither monk nor ascetic. The Self is beyond good and evil, beyond all the suffering of the human heart.

[23-30] In that unitive state one sees without seeing, for there is nothing separate from him; smells without

smelling, for there is nothing separate from him; tastes without tasting, for there is nothing separate from him; speaks without speaking, for there is nothing separate from him; hears without hearing, for there is nothing separate from him; touches without touching, for there is nothing separate from him; thinks without thinking, for there is nothing separate from him; knows without knowing, for there is nothing separate from him.

[31] Where there is separateness, one sees another, smells another, tastes another, speaks to another, hears another, touches another, thinks of another, knows another.

[32] But where there is unity, one without a second, that is the world of Brahman. This is the supreme goal of life, the supreme treasure, the supreme joy. Those who do not seek this supreme goal live on but a fraction of this joy.

JANAKA

[33] I give you another thousand cows! Please teach me more of the way to Self-realization.

YAJNAVALKYA

[35] As a heavily laden cart creaks as it moves along, the body groans under its burden when a person is about

to die. ³⁶ When the body grows weak through old age or illness, the Self separates himself as a mango or fig or banyan fruit frees itself from the stalk, and returns the way he came to begin another life.

³⁷ Just as when a king is expected to visit a village, the mayor and all the other officials turn out to welcome him with food and drink, all creation awaits the person who sheds his body having realized Brahman. "Here he comes!" they say. "Here comes Brahman himself!" ³⁸ But the senses, while that man lies dying, gather around and mourn the Self's departure, as courtiers mourn when their king is about to leave.

[4]

¹ When body and mind grow weak, the Self gathers in all the powers of life and descends with them into the heart. As prana leaves the eye, it ceases to see. ² "He is becoming one," say the wise; "he does not see. He is becoming one; he no longer hears. He is becoming one; he no longer speaks, or tastes, or smells, or thinks, or knows." By the light of the heart the Self leaves the body by one of its gates; and when he leaves, prana follows, and with it all the vital powers of the body. He who is dying merges in consciousness, and thus consciousness accompanies him when he departs,

along with the impressions of all that he has done, experienced, and known.

³ As a caterpillar, having come to the end of one blade of grass, draws itself together and reaches out for the next, so the Self, having come to the end of one life and dispelled all ignorance, gathers in his faculties and reaches out from the old body to a new.

⁴ As a goldsmith fashions an old ornament into a new and more beautiful one, so the Self, having reached the end of the last life and dispelled all ignorance, makes for himself a new, more beautiful shape, like that of the devas or other celestial beings.

⁵ The Self is indeed Brahman, but through ignorance people identify it with intellect, mind, senses, passions, and the elements of earth, water, air, space, and fire. This is why the Self is said to consist of this and that, and appears to be everything.

As a person acts, so he becomes in life. Those who do good become good; those who do harm become bad. Good deeds make one pure; bad deeds make one impure. You are what your deep, driving desire is. As your desire is, so is your will. As your will is, so is your deed. As your deed is, so is your destiny.

6 We live in accordance with our deep, driving desire. It is this desire at the time of death that determines what our next life will be. We will come back to earth to work out the satisfaction of that desire.

But not those who are free from desire; they are free because all their desires have found fulfillment in the Self. They do not die like the others; but realizing Brahman, they merge in Brahman. 7 So it is said:

When all the desires that surge in the heart
Are renounced, the mortal becomes immortal.
When all the knots that strangle the heart
Are loosened, the mortal becomes immortal,
Here in this very life.

As the skin of a snake is sloughed onto an anthill, so does the mortal body fall; but the Self, freed from the body, merges in Brahman, infinite life, eternal light.

JANAKA

I give you another thousand cows! Please teach me more of the way to Self-realization.

YAJNAVALKYA

23 Those who realize the Self enter into the peace that brings complete self-control and perfect patience. They see themselves in everyone and everyone in

themselves. Evil cannot overcome them because they overcome all evil. Sin cannot consume them because they consume all sin. Free from evil, free from sin and doubt, they live in the kingdom of Brahman. Your majesty, this kingdom is yours!

JANAKA

Venerable One, I offer myself and my kingdom in your service.

CHAPTER V

What the Thunder Said

[2]

The children of Prajapati, the Creator – gods, human beings, and asuras, the godless – lived with their father as students. When they had completed the allotted period the gods said, "Venerable One, please teach us."

Prajapati answered with one syllable: "*Da.*"

"Have you understood?" he asked.

"Yes," they said. "You have told us *damyata*, be self-controlled."

"You have understood," he said.

² Then the human beings approached. "Venerable One, please teach us."

Prajapati answered with one syllable: "*Da.*"

"Have you understood?" he asked.

"Yes," they said. "You have told us *datta*, give."

"You have understood," he said.

Then the godless approached. "Venerable One, please teach us."

Prajapati answered with the same syllable: "*Da.*"

"Have you understood?" he asked.

"Yes," they said. "You have told us *dayadhvam*, be compassionate."

"You have understood," he said.

The heavenly voice of the thunder repeats this teaching. *Da-da-da!* Be self-controlled! Give! Be compassionate!

OM *shanti shanti shanti*

◫ *The Chandogya Upanishad*

Those who depart from this world without knowing who they are or what they truly desire have no freedom here or hereafter.

But those who leave here knowing who they are and what they truly desire have freedom everywhere, both in this world and in the next.

[VIII.1.6]

INTRODUCTION

0: *Sacred Song*

IN THE WISDOM OF ANCIENT INDIA, the universe came forth from the invisible and unchanging Reality like the uttering of a meaningful sound: mystical speech (which is why the Vedas are thought of as existing long before human beings or anything else). It was not a Big Bang but a big *Om*; and it is with this image that the Upanishad named Chandogya, "the uprising of sacred song," begins. Just as Western scientists seek the laws of the physical universe in a kind of echo of that primordial explosion, the sages who predated them by so many centuries "heard" *Om,* the primordial sound, and discovered deep laws governing all existence.

The universe is founded on two principles, they discovered. One is *rita*, law, order, or regularity. Without it no scientific discovery would be possible; more importantly, no moral discovery would be possible. Human experience would have no meaning, for we would have no way to learn from our experiences.

The second principle is *yajna*, sacrifice. The universe, they tell us, runs on renunciation. The most significant human action is the sacrifice of personal gain for the sake of something higher and holier.

If rita is the moral law, yajna is the human response to live in accordance with that law, taking nothing from life for oneself but everywhere seeking to give of oneself to life. Jesus was essentially describing rita when he said, "By the same measure you mete out to others, by that measure shall it be meted out to you," and yajna when he said, "Lay not up for yourselves treasures upon earth. . . . But seek first the kingdom of God and his righteousness, and all these things shall be added unto you." We can use things, but to be in harmony with the underlying laws of life we should never feel that they are really ours: as the Isha Upanishad so simply puts it, "Everything belongs to the Lord."

This awareness leads to a profound peace, which the Chandogya conveys in one of the Upanishads' most poignant images: "As a tethered bird flies this way and that, and comes to rest at last on its own perch, so the mind, tired of wandering about . . . settles down in the Self" (VI.8.2). This Upanishad charts an inward course back to speech, breath, and vital energy (prana), and ultimately to the Self, or Brahman. Prana tends to become the focus of attention whenever it comes up, and that is what happens in the sections that follow containing the famous stories of Satyakama (IV.4) and Shvetaketu (VII). These two spiritual students are a striking contrast, as

Satyakama breaks social convention: born out of wedlock, he has the courage to admit as much to his teacher, who honors that courage and accepts him. This episode is one of the most imaginative frame stories for teaching in all the Upanishads (which is saying a lot), as various odd birds and animals teach him "one foot of Brahman" at a time until he is illumined.

Prana also provides an explanation for the process we call death, as prana, life-energy, is withdrawn by progressive steps – the same kind of steps by which the universe itself was manifested and will be withdrawn – into its ultimate source (VI.15). This prepares us for the triumphant declaration of Chapter VIII, the "City of Brahman," a moving description of Brahmaloka, the "Land of No Change" beyond all death and suffering. While we actually visit this state without knowing it while in deep sleep (VI.8.1 and VIII.3.2), we can possess it in full awareness through the heroic spiritual disciplines the Upanishads are always leading us to. We can live in this very world free from sorrow, ill health, perturbation, distress of any kind; and then for us death, while it claims the body, will never touch us because we are identified completely with the Self, which is a "bridge" or "bulwark" (VIII.4) none of these can cross.

– M . N .

Lead me from the unreal to the Real.
Lead me from darkness to light.
Lead me from death to immortality.

OM *shanti shanti shanti*

II: *The Chandogya Upanishad*

CHAPTER I

The Word

1.1 Let us meditate on O M the imperishable, the beginning of prayer.

2 For as the earth comes from the waters, plants from earth, and man from plants, so man is speech, and speech is O M. Of all speech the essence is the Rig Veda; but Sama is the essence of Rig, and of Sama the essence is O M, the Udgitha.

3 This is the essence of essences, the highest, the eighth rung, venerated above all that human beings hold holy. O M is the Self of all.

4 What is *rig,* what is *sama,* at the heart of prayer? **5** As *rig* is speech, so *sama* is song, and the imperishable O M is the Udgitha. Speech and breath, Sama and Rig, are couples,**6** and in the imperishable O M they come together to fulfill each other's desire. 7 For those who, knowing this, meditate on the imperishable O M, all desires are fulfilled. 8 With the word O M we say, "I agree," and fulfill desires.9 With O M we recite, we give direction, we sing aloud the honor of that Word, the key to the three kinds of knowledge. 10 Side by side, those who know the Self and those who know it not do the same thing; but it is not the same: the act done with knowledge, with inner awareness and faith, grows in power. That, in a word, tells the significance of O M, the indivisible.

CHAPTER III
The Wisdom of Shandilya

14.1 This universe comes forth from Brahman, exists in Brahman, and will return to Brahman. Verily, all is Brahman.

A person is what his deep desire is. It is our deepest desire in this life that shapes the life to come. So let us direct our deepest desires to realize the Self.

14.2 The Self, who can be realized by the pure in heart, who is life, light, truth, space, who gives rise to all works, all desires, all odors, all tastes, who is beyond words, who is joy abiding – 14.3 this is the Self dwelling in my heart.

Smaller than a grain of rice, smaller than a grain of barley, smaller than a mustard seed, smaller than a grain of millet, smaller even than the kernel of a grain of millet is the Self. This is the Self dwelling in my heart, greater than the earth, greater than the sky, greater than all the worlds.

14.4 This Self who gives rise to all works, all desires, all odors, all tastes, who pervades the universe, who is beyond words, who is joy abiding, who is ever present in my heart, is Brahman indeed. To him I shall attain when my ego dies.

So said Shandilya; so said Shandilya.

CHAPTER IV
The Story of Satyakama

4.1 "Mother," Satyakama said, "I feel the time has come for me to go to the home of a spiritual teacher. From whom does our family come, so that I may tell him when he asks my lineage?"

4.2 "I do not know, dear," she replied. "You were born when I was young and going from place to place as a servant. Your name is Satyakama and my name is Jabala; why not call yourself Satyakama Jabala?"

4.3 Satyakama went to Haridrumata Gautama and said to him, "Sir, I want to become your disciple."

4.4 "What family are you from, bright one?"

"Sir, I don't know. My mother says she bore me in her youth and doesn't know my ancestry. She says that since my name is Satyakama and hers is Jabala I should call myself Satyakama Jabala."

4.5 "None but a true brahmin could have said that. Fetch the firewood, my boy; I will initiate you. You have not flinched from the truth."

He selected four hundred lean and sickly cows and gave them to Satyakama to care for. "I shall not return," the boy said to himself, "until they become a thousand."

5.1 For years Satyakama dwelt in the forest, tending the herd. Then one day the bull of the herd said to him: "Satyakama!"

"Sir?" he replied.

"We have become a thousand. Let us now rejoin our

teacher's family, **5.2** and I will tell you one of the four feet of Brahman."

"Please tell me, revered sir," the boy said.

"There are four quarters: east, west, south, and north.
This is one foot of Brahman, called the Shining.
To meditate on these four is to become full of light
and master the resplendent regions of the cosmos,
knowing this portion of the truth. **6.1** Agni, fire, will
tell you more."

The next day Satyakama set out for his teacher's house
with the herd. Toward evening he made a fire, penned
the cows, and sat by the fire facing east. **6.2** The fire
spoke: "Satyakama!"

"Sir?"

6.3 "Friend, I can teach you another foot of Brahman."

"Please do, revered sir."

"There are four quarters: earth, sky, heaven, and
ocean. This is one foot of Brahman, called Without
End. Know this, meditate on this reality, and your life
will be without end on this earth. **7.1** A swan will tell
you more."

The next day Satyakama drove the cows onward.
Toward evening he lit a fire, penned the cows, and sat
by the fire facing east. **7.2** Then a swan flew near and
said: "Satyakama!"

"Sir?"

7.3 "Friend, I can teach you another foot of Brahman."

"Please do, revered sir."

"There are four quarters: fire, the sun, the moon, and
lightning. These make one foot of Brahman, called
Full of Light. **7.4** To meditate on this fourfold foot of
truth is to be filled with light in this world and master
the world of light. **8.1** A diver bird will tell you more."

The next day Satyakama drove the cows onward.
Toward evening he lit a fire, penned the cows, and sat
by the fire facing east. **8.2** Then a diver bird flew near
and spoke to him: "Satyakama!"

"Sir?"

8.3 "Friend, I can teach you another foot of Brahman."

"Please do, revered sir."

"There are four parts: breath, eye, ear, and mind.
This is one foot of Brahman, called Established. **8.4** To

meditate on this fourfold foot of Brahman is to be at home in this world and master space. Whoever knows this fourfold foot of Brahman is called established."

9.1 So Satyakama returned to his teacher's home. "Satyakama," his teacher called, **9.2** "you glow like one who has known the truth. Tell me, who has taught you?"

Satyakama replied, "No human, sir. But I wish to hear the truth from you alone. **9.3** For I have heard that only the teacher's wisdom comes to fruition for us."

Then his teacher taught Satyakama that same wisdom. Nothing was left out from it; nothing was left out.

CHAPTER VI
The Story of Shvetaketu

1.1 Shvetaketu was Uddalaka's son.
When he was twelve, his father said to him:
"It is time for you to find a teacher,
Dear one, for no one in our family
Is a stranger to the spiritual life."

1.2 So Shvetaketu went to a teacher
And studied all the Vedas for twelve years.

At the end of this time he returned home,
Proud of his intellectual knowledge.

"You seem to be proud of all this learning,"
Said Uddalaka. "But did you ask
Your teacher for that spiritual wisdom
1.3 Which enables you to hear the unheard,
Think the unthought, and know the unknown?"

"What is that wisdom, Father?" asked the son.

Uddalaka said to Shvetaketu:
1.4 "As by knowing one lump of clay, dear one,
We come to know all things made out of clay
That they differ only in name and form,
While the stuff of which all are made is clay;
1.5 As by knowing one gold nugget, dear one,
We come to know all things made out of gold:
That they differ only in name and form,
While the stuff of which all are made is gold;
1.6 As by knowing one tool of iron, dear one,
We come to know all things made out of iron:
That they differ only in name and form,
While the stuff of which all are made is iron –
So through that spiritual wisdom, dear one,
We come to know that all of life is one."

1.7 "My teachers must not have known this wisdom,"
Said Shvetaketu, "for if they had known,
How could they have failed to teach it to me? Please
instruct me in this wisdom, Father."

"Yes, dear one, I will," replied his father.

2.2 "In the beginning was only Being,
One without a second.
2.3 Out of himself he brought forth the cosmos
And entered into everything in it.
There is nothing that does not come from him.
Of everything he is the inmost Self.
He is the truth; he is the Self supreme.
You are that, Shvetaketu; you are that."

"Please, Father, tell me more about this Self."

"Yes, dear one, I will," Uddalaka said.

8.1 "Let us start with sleep. What happens in it?
When one is absorbed in dreamless sleep,
He is one with the Self, though he knows it not.
We say he sleeps, but he sleeps in the Self.
8.2 As a tethered bird grows tired of flying
About in vain to find a place of rest
And settles down at last on its own perch,
So the mind, tired of wandering about

Hither and thither, settles down at last

In the Self, dear one, to which it is bound.

8.4 All creatures, dear one, have their source in him.

He is their home; he is their strength."

8.6 "When a person departs from this world, dear one,

His speech merges in mind, his mind in prana,

Prana in fire, and fire in pure Being.

8.7 There is nothing that does not come from him.

Of everything he is the inmost Self.

He is the truth; he is the Self supreme.

You are that, Shvetaketu; you are that."

"Please tell me, Father, more about this Self."

"Yes, dear one, I will," Uddalaka said.

9.1 "As bees suck nectar from many a flower

And make their honey one, 9.2 so that no drop

Can say, "I am from this flower or that,"

All creatures, though one, know not they are that One.

9.3 There is nothing that does not come from him.

Of everything he is the inmost Self.

He is the truth; he is the Self supreme.

You are that, Shvetaketu; you are that."

"Please, Father, tell me more about this Self."

"Yes, dear one, I will," Uddalaka said.

10.1 "As the rivers flowing east and west

Merge in the sea and become one with it,

Forgetting they were ever separate rivers,

10.2 So do all creatures lose their separateness

When they merge at last into pure Being.

10.3 There is nothing that does not come from him.

Of everything he is the inmost Self.

He is the truth; he is the Self supreme.

You are that, Shvetaketu; you are that."

"Please, Father, tell me more about this Self."

"Yes, dear one, I will," Uddalaka said.

11.1 "Strike at the root of a tree; it would bleed

But still live. Strike at the trunk; it would bleed

But still live. Strike again at the top;

It would bleed but still live. The Self as life

Supports the tree, which stands firm and enjoys

The nourishment it receives.

11.2 If the Self leaves one branch, that branch withers.

If it leaves a second, that too withers.

If it leaves a third, that again withers.

Let it leave the whole tree, the whole tree dies.

11.3 Just so, dear one, when death comes and the Self

Departs from the body, the body dies.

But the Self dies not."

"There is nothing that does not come from him.
Of everything he is the inmost Self.
He is the truth; he is the Self supreme.
You are that, Shvetaketu; you are that."

"Please, Father, tell me more about this Self."

"Yes, dear one, I will," Uddalaka said.
12.1 "Bring me a fruit from the nyagrodha tree."

"Here it is, sir."

"Break it. What do you see?"

"These seeds, Father, all exceedingly small."

"Break one. What do you see?"

"Nothing at all."

12.2 "That hidden essence you do not see, dear one,
From that a whole *nyagrodha* tree will grow.
12.3 There is nothing that does not come from him.
Of everything he is the inmost Self.
He is the truth; he is the Self supreme.
You are that, Shvetaketu; you are that."

"Please, Father, tell me more about this Self."

"Yes, dear one, I will," Uddalaka said.
13.1 "Place this salt in water and bring it here

Tomorrow morning." The boy did.
"Where is that salt?" his father asked.

"I do not see it."

13.2 "Sip here. How does it taste?"

"Salty, Father."

"And here? And there?"

"I taste salt everywhere."

"It *is* everywhere, though we see it not.
Just so, dear one, the Self is everywhere,
Within all things, although we see him not.
13.3 There is nothing that does not come from him.
Of everything he is the inmost Self.
He is the truth; he is the Self supreme.
You are that, Shvetaketu; you are that."

"Please, Father, tell me more about this Self."

"Yes, dear one, I will," Uddalaka said.

14.1 "As a man from Gandhara, blindfolded,
Led away and left in a lonely place,
Turns to the east and west and north and south
And shouts, 'I am left here and cannot see!'
14.2 Until one removes his blindfold and says,

'There lies Gandhara; follow that path,'
And thus informed, able to see for himself,
The man inquires from village to village
And reaches his homeland at last – just so,
My son, one who finds an illumined teacher
Attains to spiritual wisdom in the Self.
14.3 There is nothing that does not come from him.
Of everything he is the inmost Self.
He is the truth; he is the Self supreme.
You are that, Shvetaketu; you are that."

"Please, Father, tell me more about this Self."

"Yes, dear one, I will," Uddalaka said.

15.1 "When a man is dying, his family
All gather round and ask, 'Do you know me?
Do you know me?' And so long as his speech
Has not merged in mind, his mind in prana,
Prana in fire, and fire in pure Being,
15.2 He knows them all. But there is no more knowing
When speech merges in mind, mind in prana,
Prana in fire, and fire in pure Being,
15.3 There is nothing that does not come from him.
Of everything he is the inmost Self.
He is the truth; he is the Self supreme.
You are that, Shvetaketu; you are that."

16.3 Then Shvetaketu understood this teaching;
Truly he understood it all.

CHAPTER VII

Narada's Education

1.1 Narada approached the sage Sanatkumara and said, "Please teach me, Venerable One."

"Tell me what you know," replied the sage, "and then I will teach you what is beyond that."

1.2 "I know the four Vedas – Rig, Yajur, Sama, Atharva – and the epics, called the fifth. I have studied grammar, rituals, mathematics, astronomy, logic, economics, physics, psychology, the fine arts, and even snake-charming. **1.3** But all this knowledge has not helped me to know the Self. I have heard from spiritual teachers like you that one who realizes the Self goes beyond sorrow. I am lost in sorrow. Please teach me how to go beyond."

"Whatever you know is just words," said Sanatkumara, "names of finite phenomena. **23.1** It is the Infinite that is the source of abiding joy because it is not subject to change. Therefore seek to know the Infinite."

"I seek to know the Infinite, Venerable One."

24.1 "Where one realizes the indivisible unity of life, sees nothing else, hears nothing else, knows nothing else, that is the Infinite. Where one sees separateness, hears separateness, knows separateness, that is the finite. The Infinite is beyond death, but the finite cannot escape death."

"On what does the Infinite depend, Venerable One?"

"On its own glory – no, not even on that. **24.2** In the world people think they can attain glory by having cows and horses, elephants and gold, family and servants, fields and mansions. But I do not call that glory, for here one thing depends on another. Utterly independent is the Infinite.

25.1 "The Infinite is above and below, before and behind, to the right and to the left. I am all this. The Self is above and below, before and behind, to the right and to the left. I am all this. **25.2** One who meditates upon the Self and realizes the Self sees the Self everywhere, and rejoices in the Self. Such a one lives in freedom and is at home wherever he goes. But those who pursue the finite are blind to the Self and live in bondage.

26.1 "One who meditates upon and realizes the Self discovers that everything in the cosmos – energy and space, fire and water, name and form, birth and death, mind and will, word and deed, mantram and meditation – all come from the Self.

26.2 "The Self is one, though it appears to be many. Those who meditate upon the Self and realize the Self go beyond decay and death, beyond separateness and sorrow. They see the Self in everyone and obtain all things.

"Control the senses and purify the mind. In a pure mind there is constant awareness of the Self. Where there is constant awareness of the Self, freedom ends bondage and joy ends sorrow."

Thus the sage Sanatkumara taught the pure Narada to go beyond bondage, beyond sorrow, beyond darkness, to the light of the Self.

CHAPTER VIII
The City of Brahman

1.1 In the city of Brahman is a secret dwelling, the lotus of the heart. Within this dwelling is a space, and within that space is the fulfillment of our desires. What is within that space should be longed for and realized.

1.3 As great as the infinite space beyond is the space within the lotus of the heart. Both heaven and earth are contained in that inner space, both fire and air, sun and moon, lightning and stars. Whether we know it in this world or know it not, everything is contained in that inner space.

1.5 Never fear that old age will invade that city; never fear that this inner treasure of all reality will wither and decay. This knows no age when the body ages; this knows no dying when the body dies. This is the real city of Brahman; this is the Self, free from old age, from death and grief, hunger and thirst. In the Self all desires are fulfilled.

The Self desires only what is real, thinks nothing but what is true. Here people do what they are told, becoming dependent on their country, or their piece of land, or the desires of another, **1.6** so their desires are not fulfilled and their works come to nothing, both in this world and in the next. Those who depart from this world without knowing who they are or what they truly desire have no freedom here or hereafter.

But those who leave here knowing who they are and what they truly desire have freedom everywhere, both in this world and in the next.

1.1-2 Would they see their departed mother or father? Lo, they see them and are happy. **1.3-6** Would they see their family and friends? Lo, they see them and are happy. Would they enjoy the world of music, of spring flowers, of elegance? Lo, by their mere will they enjoy these things. **1.10** Whatever they desire, the object of that desire arises from the power of their own thoughts; they have it and are happy.

3.1 Here our selfless desires are hidden by selfish ones. They are real, but they are covered by what is false. Therefore whoever of our own departs from this life, not one can ever be brought back before our eyes. **3.2** But all those we love, alive or departed, and all things we desire but do not have, are found when we enter that space within the heart; for there abide all desires that are true, though covered by what is false.

Like strangers in an unfamiliar country walking over a hidden treasure, day by day we enter the world of Brahman while in deep sleep but never find it, carried away by what is false.

3.3 The Self is hidden in the lotus of the heart. Those who see themselves in all creatures go day by day into the world of Brahman hidden in the heart. **4** Established in peace, they rise above body-consciousness to the supreme light of the Self. Immortal, free from fear, this Self is Brahman, called the True. 5 Beyond the mortal and the immortal, he binds both worlds together. Those who know this live day after day in heaven in this very life.

4.1 The Self is a bulwark against the confounding of these worlds and a bridge between them. Day and night cannot cross that bridge, nor old age, nor death, nor grief, nor evil nor good deeds. All evils turn back there, unable to cross; evil comes not into this world of Brahman.

4.2 One who crosses by this bridge, if blind, is blind no more; if hurt, ceases to be hurt; if in sorrow, ceases sorrowing. At this boundary night itself becomes day: night comes not into this world of Brahman.

4.3 Only those who are pure and self-controlled can find this world of Brahman. That world is theirs alone. In that world, in all the worlds, they live in perfect freedom.

The Gods and the Godless

7.1 The great teacher Prajapati said: "The Self is pure, free from decay and death, free from hunger and thirst, and free from sorrow. The Self desires nothing

that is not good, wills nothing that is not good. Seek
and realize the Self! Those who seek and realize the
Self fulfill all their desires and attain the goal supreme."

7.2 The devas and the asuras, the gods and the godless,
heard this truth and said: "Let us seek and realize the
Self so that we may fulfill all our desires." So Indra
from among the gods and Virochana from among
the godless approached Prajapati, carrying fuel in
their hands as a sign that they wanted to become his
disciples. 7.3 They dwelt with him for thirty-two years,
and at the end of that time Prajapati asked why they
had stayed with him so long.

Indra and Virochana replied, "We have heard of your
inspiring words: 'The Self is pure, free from decay
and death, free from hunger and thirst, and free from
sorrow. The Self desires nothing that is not good, wills
nothing that is not good. Seek and realize the Self!
Those who seek and realize the Self fulfill all their
desires and attain the goal supreme.' We have been
living here as your disciples because we want to realize
the Self."

7.4 Prajapati said to them: "When you look into
another's eyes, what you see is the Self, fearless and
deathless. That is Brahman, the supreme."

"Venerable One," asked the two disciples, "what is it we see reflected in the water or in a mirror?"

"It is the Self you see in all these," he said to them. 8.1 "Now look at yourself in a bowl of water, and ask me anything you want to learn about the Self."

They looked at themselves in a bowl of water.

"What did you see in the water?"

"We have seen the Self, even the hair and the nails."

8.2 "Put on your best clothes, adorn your body, and look again in the water."

They did so, and came back to Prajapati.

"What did you see in the water?" he asked.

8.3 "We have seen the Self, well dressed and well adorned," they replied.

"That is the Self, fearless and deathless. That is Brahman, the supreme."

Indra and Virochana went away satisfied. 8.4 But Prajapati said to himself: "They have seen the Self, but they have not recognized the Self. They mistake the Self to be the body. Those who think the Self is the body will lose their way in life."

Virochana, quite sure that the Self is the body, went back to the godless and began to teach them that the body alone is to be saved, the body alone is to be adored. He taught them that whoever lives for indulging the senses will find joy in this world and the next. **8.5** Even today people are called godless when they lack faith, love, and charity, because that is the way of the godless. They dress even dead bodies in fine clothes and adorn them with ornaments so that they may enjoy their life in the next world.

9.1 But Indra, as he was on his way home to the gathering of the gods, began to question this knowledge. "If the Self is the same as the body, well dressed when the body is well dressed, well adorned when the body is well adorned, then the Self will be blind when the body is blind, lame when the body is lame, paralyzed when the body is paralyzed. And when the body dies, the Self too will die. In such knowledge I see no value."

9.2 Again Indra went back to Prajapati with fuel in hand.

"Why have you returned, Indra?" his teacher asked. "Did you not go away quite satisfied?"

"Venerable One," replied Indra, "if the Self is well dressed when the body is well dressed, well adorned

when the body is well adorned, then the Self will be
blind when the body is blind, lame when the body
is lame, paralyzed when the body is paralyzed. And
when the body dies, the Self too will die. In such
knowledge I see no value."

9.3 "You are thinking clearly, Indra," said Prajapati.
"Live with me for another thirty-two years and I will
teach you more of the Self."

So Indra lived with Prajapati for another thirty-two
years. Then Prajapati said to him: 10.1 "That which
moves about in joy in the dreaming state is the Self,
fearless and deathless. That is Brahman, the supreme."

Indra went away satisfied, but on his way home to
the gathering of the gods he began to question this
knowledge. "In the dreaming state, it is true, the Self
is not blind when the body is blind, nor lame when
the body is lame, nor paralyzed when the body is
paralyzed, 10.2 nor slain when the body is slain. Yet in
dreams the Self may appear to suffer and to be slain; it
may become conscious of pain and even weep. In such
knowledge I see no value."

10.3 Again Indra went back to Prajapati with fuel in
hand.

"Why have you returned, Indra?" his teacher asked. "Did you not go away quite satisfied?"

"Venerable One," replied Indra, "in the dreaming state, it is true, the Self is not blind when the body is blind, nor lame when the body is lame; yet in this state the Self may still suffer and even weep. In such knowledge I see no value."

10.4 "You are thinking clearly, Indra," said Prajapati. "Live with me for another thirty-two years and I will teach you more of the Self."

Indra lived with Prajapati for another thirty-two years. Then his teacher said:

11.1 "When a person is sleeping soundly, free from dreams, with a still mind, that is the Self, fearless and deathless. That is Brahman, the supreme."

Indra went away satisfied, but on his way home to the gathering of the gods he began to question this knowledge. "In the state of dreamless sleep one is not aware of oneself or any other. The state of dreamless sleep is very close to extinction. In this knowledge I see no value."

11.2 Again Indra went back to Prajapati with fuel in hand.

"Why have you returned, Indra?" his teacher asked. "Did you not go away quite satisfied?"

"Venerable One", replied Indra, "in the state of dreamless sleep one is not aware of oneself or of any other. The state of dreamless sleep is very close to extinction. In this knowledge I see no value."

11.3 "You are thinking clearly, Indra," said Prajapati. "Live with me for another five years and I will teach you to realize the Self."

Indra lived with Prajapati for another five years. Altogether he lived with his teacher for one hundred and one years, which is why people say, "Even Indra had to live with his teacher for one hundred and one years." After that time, Prajapati revealed the highest truth of the Self to Indra:

12.1 "It is true the body is perishable, but within it dwells the imperishable Self. This body is subject to pleasure and pain; no one who identifies with the body can escape from pleasure and pain. But those who know they are not the body pass beyond pleasure and pain to live in abiding joy.

¹²·² "Like the wind, like clouds, like thunder and lightning, which rise from space without physical shape and reach the transcendent light in their own form, those who rise above body-consciousness ascend to the transcendent light in their real form, the Self.

"In that state, free from attachment, they move at will, laughing, playing, and rejoicing. They know the Self is not this body, but only tied to it for a time as an ox is tied to its cart. Whenever one sees, smells, speaks, hears, or thinks, they know it is the Self that sees, smells, speaks, hears, and thinks; the senses are but his instruments.

"Worshipping this Self in the world of Brahman, the gods obtained all worlds and all desires. Those who know this Self and realize this Self obtain all worlds and all desires." So said Prajapati; so taught Prajapati.

A Paean of Illumination

¹³·¹ From the Divine Dark to the manifest
To the Divine Dark I pass again.
As a horse shakes free its mane, I have
Shaken off all evil. Freeing myself
From the bonds of birth and death as the moon

Escapes from Rahu's mouth, I have attained
The pure realm of Brahman; I have attained
The pure realm of Brahman.

15.1 Brahman is my home. I shall not lose it.
Truly I shall not be lost again.

OM *shanti shanti shanti*

11: The Shvetashvatara Upanishad

The Lord dwells in the womb of the cosmos,
The creator who is in all creatures.
He is that which is born and to be born;
His face is everywhere.

[11.16]

❑: *The Faces of God*

HOW DOES THE ONE CHANGELESS Reality become the myriad phenomena that make up the observable world? This question could be asked by a contemporary physicist; but here it is posed by an ancient seeker after wisdom, which gives it a slightly different "take" and a different answer.

Like the Isha, the Shvetashvatara is unusual among Upanishads in the emphasis – let us say the loving attention – it places on a personal God. In this respect, in fact, it goes one step further than the Isha. It begins by addressing the Supreme Being with the Vedic terms Rudra and Isha or Ishvara, but soon enough introduces the actual name of Shiva, who has been for so many centuries the focus of intense personal devotion throughout India.

The impressive fact is how little difference it makes in the Upanishadic approach whether the emphasis falls on personal or impersonal. The personal note struck by the Shvetashvatara does nothing to jar the Upanishadic spirit. Sri

Ramakrishna used to say that just as water congeals into ice, the Ocean of Reality can be frozen into a provisional form by the devotee's needs, but it is still the same substance.

This devotional character, and the fact that it is entirely a verse Upanishad, marks the Shvetashvatara as relatively late. Another mark is the inclusion of certain concepts and nomenclature that we associate with later philosophical schools like classical Sankhya. Some see in this an attempt to reconcile early Sankhya with other philosophical and religious tendencies of the time; but it does show how the lofty vision of the Upanishads was a kind of mother lode from which the philosophical schools took off on their respective intellectual adventures.

Like all the Upanishads, the Shvetashvatara is a paean of ecstasy to the Self, the Reality "hidden behind the gunas" but seen by sages in the depths of their meditation. To be grounded in this experience is the only reliable ground in a universe which is so confusing, as we can sense in the intense opening questions – questions that have resounded throughout human history. The Upanishads are never interested in such matters from a merely objective standpoint. The thrust of these questions is intensely personal: how does this world of separateness, with its inescapable forces of pain and pleasure, so intricately entangle us? The Upanishad's answer is *maya*. The objective world is neither real nor unreal; it is appearance – specifically, the appearance of separateness, the illusion that happiness comes from the world outside rather than from within us. The Shvetashvatara is an early witness to this powerful concept (1.9). Maya was the cornerstone of Shankara's system, and he wrote a special commentary on this Upanishad. It remains a concept that, when grasped, can be liberating to the spirit and satisfying to the mind of any earnest puzzler over reality.

— M . N .

All this is full. All that is full.
From fullness, fullness comes.
When fullness is taken from fullness,
Fullness still remains.

O M *shanti shanti shanti*

II: *The Shvetashvatara Upanishad*

[1]

1 What is the cause of the cosmos? Is it Brahman?
From where do we come? By what live?
Where shall we find peace at last?
What power governs the duality
Of pleasure and pain by which we are driven?

2 Time, nature, necessity, accident,
Elements, energy, intelligence –
None of these can be the First Cause.
They are effects, whose only purpose is
To help the self rise above pleasure and pain.

3 In the depths of meditation, sages
Saw within themselves the Lord of Love,
Who dwells in the heart of every creature.
Deep in the hearts of all he dwells, hidden
Behind the gunas of law, energy,

And inertia. He is One. He it is
Who rules over time, space, and causality.

4 The world is the wheel of God, turning round
And round with all living creatures upon its rim.
5 The world is the river of God,
Flowing from him and flowing back to him.

6 On this ever-revolving wheel of life
The individual self goes round and round
Through life after life, believing itself
To be a separate creature, until
It sees its identity with the Lord of Love
And attains immortality in the indivisible whole.

7 He is the eternal reality, sing
The scriptures, and the ground of existence.
Those who perceive him in every creature
Merge in him and are released from the wheel
Of birth and death.

8 The Lord of Love holds in his hand the world,
Composed of the changing and the changeless,
The manifest and the unmanifest.
The separate self, not yet aware of the Lord,
Goes after pleasure, only to become
Bound more and more. When it sees the Lord,
There comes an end to its bondage.

⁹ Conscious spirit and unconscious matter
Both have existed since the dawn of time,
With maya appearing to connect them,
Misrepresenting joy as outside us.
When all these three are seen as one, the Self
Reveals his universal form and serves
As an instrument of the divine will.

¹⁰ All is change in the world of the senses,
But changeless is the supreme Lord of Love.
Meditate on him, be absorbed in him,
Wake up from this dream of separateness.

¹¹ Know God and all fetters will fall away.
No longer identifying yourself
With the body, go beyond birth and death.
All your desires will be fulfilled in him
Who is One without a second.

¹² Know him to be enshrined in your heart always.
Truly there is nothing more in life to know.
Meditate and realize that this world
Is filled with the presence of God.

¹³ Fire is not seen until one firestick rubs
Against another, though the fire remains
Hidden in the firestick. So does the Lord

Remain hidden in the body until

He is revealed through the mystic mantram.

14 Let your body be the lower firestick;

Let the mantram be the upper. Rub them

Against each other in meditation

And realize the Lord.

15 Like oil in sesame seeds, like butter

In cream, like water in springs, like fire

In firesticks, so dwells the Lord of Love,

The Self, in the very depths of consciousness.

Realize him through truth and meditation.

16 The Self is hidden in the hearts of all,

As butter lies hidden in cream. Realize

The Self in the depths of meditation,

The Lord of Love, supreme reality,

Who is the goal of all knowledge.

This is the highest mystical teaching;

This is the highest mystical teaching.

[11]

1 May we harness body and mind to see

The Lord of Life, who dwells in everyone.

2 May we ever with a one-pointed mind

Strive for blissful union with the Lord.
³ May we train our senses to serve the Lord
Through the practice of meditation.

⁴ Great is the glory of the Lord of Life,
Infinite, omnipresent, all-knowing.
He is known by the wise who meditate
And conserve their vital energy.

⁵ Hear, O children of immortal bliss!
You are born to be united with the Lord.
Follow the path of the illumined ones
And be united with the Lord of Life.

⁶ Kindle the fire of kundalini deep
In meditation. Bring your mind and breath
Under control. Drink deep of divine love,
And you will attain the unitive state.

⁷ Dedicate yourself to the Lord of Life,
Who is the cause of the cosmos. He will
Remove the cause of all your suffering
And free you from the bondage of karma.

⁸ Be seated with spinal column erect
And turn your mind and senses deep within.
With the mantram echoing in your heart,
Cross over the dread sea of birth and death.

⁹ Train your senses to be obedient.
Regulate your activities to lead you
To the goal. Hold the reins of your mind
As you hold the reins of restive horses.

¹⁰ Choose a place for meditation that is
Clean, quiet, and cool, a cave with a smooth floor
Without stones and dust, protected against
Wind and rain and pleasing to the eye.

¹¹ In deep meditation aspirants may
See forms like snow or smoke. They may feel
A strong wind blowing or a wave of heat.
They may see within them more and more light:
Fireflies, lightning, sun, or moon. These are signs
That they are well on their way to Brahman.

¹²⁻¹³ Health, a light body, freedom from cravings,
A glowing skin, sonorous voice, fragrance
Of body: these signs indicate progress
In the practice of meditation.

¹⁴ As a dusty mirror shines bright when cleansed,
So shine those who realize the Self,
Attain life's goal, and pass beyond all sorrow.
¹⁵ In the supreme climax of samadhi
They realize the presence of the Lord

Within their heart. Freed from impurities,
They pass forever beyond birth and death.

16 The Lord dwells in the womb of the cosmos,
The Creator who is in all creatures.
He is that which is born and to be born;
His face is everywhere.

17 Let us adore the Lord of Life, who is
Present in fire and water, plants and trees.
Let us adore the Lord of Life!
Let us adore the Lord of Life!

[III]

1 Brahman, attributeless Reality,
Becomes the Lord of Love who casts his net
Of appearance over the cosmos and rules
It from within through his divine power.
He was before creation; he will be
After dissolution. He alone is.
Those who know him become immortal.

2 The Lord of Love is one. There is indeed
No other. He is the inner ruler
In all beings. He projects the cosmos
From himself, maintains and withdraws it
Back into himself at the end of time.

³ His eyes, mouths, arms, and feet are everywhere.
Projecting the cosmos out of himself,
He holds it all together.

⁴ He is the source of all the powers of life.
He is the lord of all, the great seer
Who dwells forever in the cosmic womb.
May he purify our consciousness!

⁵ O Lord, in whom alone we can find peace,
May we see your divine Self and be freed
From all impure thoughts and all fear.

⁶ O Lord, from whom we receive the mantram
As a weapon to destroy our self-will,
Reveal yourself, protector of all.

⁷ You are the supreme Brahman, infinite,
Yet hidden in the hearts of all creatures.
You pervade everything. Realizing you,
We attain immortality.

⁸ I have realized the Lord of Love,
Who is the sun that dispels our darkness.
Those who realize him go beyond death;
No other way is there to immortality.

⁹ There is nothing higher than him, nothing other
Than him. His infinity is beyond great

And small. In his own glory rooted,
He stands and fills the cosmos.

10 He fills the cosmos, yet he transcends it.
Those who know him leave all separateness,
Sorrow, and death behind. Those who know him not
Live but to suffer.

11 The Lord of Love, omnipresent, dwelling
In the heart of every living creature,
All mercy, turns every face to himself.

12 He is the supreme Lord, who through his grace
Moves us to seek him in our own hearts.
He is the light that shines forever.

13 He is the inner Self of all,
Hidden like a little flame in the heart.
Only by the stilled mind can he be known.
Those who realize him become immortal.

14 He has thousands of heads, thousands of eyes,
Thousands of feet; he surrounds the cosmos
15 On every side. This infinite being
Is ever present in the hearts of all.
He has become the cosmos. He is what was
And what will be. Yet he is unchanging,
The lord of immortality.

¹⁶ His hands and feet are everywhere; his heads
And mouths everywhere. He sees everything,
Hears everything, and pervades everything.

¹⁷ Without organs of sense, he shines through them.
He is the lord of all, inner ruler,
Protector and friend of all.

¹⁸ He resides in the city with nine gates,
Which is the body. He moves in the world
Enjoying the play of his countless forms.
He is the master of the universe,
Of animate and inanimate.

¹⁹ He runs without feet and holds without hands.
He sees without eyes and hears without ears.
He knows everyone, but no one knows him.
He is called the First, the Great, the Supreme.

²⁰ The Lord of Love is hidden in the heart
Of every creature, subtler than the subtlest,
Greater than the greatest. Through his grace
One sheds all selfish desires and sorrow
And becomes united with the Self.

²¹ I know this Self, sage Shvetashvatara said,
To be immortal and infinite.

I know this Self who is the Self of all,
Whom the sages call the Eternal One.

[IV]

1 May the Lord of Love, who projects himself
Into this universe of myriad forms,
From whom all beings come and to whom all
Return – may he grant us the grace of wisdom.

2 He is fire and the sun, and the moon
And the stars. He is the air and the sea,
And the Creator, Prajapati.

3 He is this boy, he is that girl, he is
This man, he is that woman, and he is
This old man, too, tottering on his staff.
His face is everywhere.

4 He is the blue bird; he is the green bird
With red eyes; he is the thundercloud,
And he is the seasons and the seas.
He has no beginning; he has no end.
He is the source from whom the worlds evolve.

5 From his divine power comes forth all this
Magical show of name and form, of you
And me, which casts the spell of pain and pleasure.

Only when we pierce through this magic veil
Do we see the One who appears as many.

⁶ Two birds of beautiful plumage, comrades
Inseparable, live on the selfsame tree.
One bird eats the fruit of pleasure and pain;
The other looks on without eating.

⁷ Forgetting our divine origin,
We become ensnared in the world of change
And bewail our helplessness. But when
We see the Lord of Love in all his glory,
Adored by all, we go beyond sorrow.

⁸ What use are the scriptures to anyone
Who knows not the one source from whom they come,
In whom all gods and worlds abide?
Only those who realize him as ever present
Within the heart attain abiding joy.

⁹ The Lord, who is the supreme magician,
Brings forth out of himself all the scriptures,
Oblations, sacrifices, spiritual disciplines,
Past and present, and the whole universe.
Invisible through the magic of maya,
He remains hidden in the hearts of all.

10 Know him to be the supreme magician
Who has brought all the worlds out of himself.
Know that all beings in the universe
Partake of his divine splendor.

11 Know him to be the supreme magician
Who has become boy and girl, bird and beast.
He is the bestower of all blessings,
And his grace fills the heart with peace profound.

12 Know him to be the supreme source of all
The gods, sole support of the universe,
The sower of the golden seed of life.
May he grant us the grace of wisdom.

13 Know him to be the supreme God of gods
From whom all the worlds draw the breath of life.
He rules every creature from within.
May he be worshipped by everyone.

14 Know him to be the supreme pervader,
In whom the whole universe is smaller
Than the smallest atom. May he, Shiva,
Fill our hearts with infinite peace.

15 Know him to be the supreme guardian
Of the cosmos, protecting all creatures

From within. May he, Shiva, in whom all
Are one, free us from the bonds of death.

16 Know him to be the Supreme One, hidden
Within the hearts of all like cream in milk
And yet encompassing the universe.
May he, Shiva, free us from all bondage.

17 Know him to be the supreme architect
Who is enshrined within the hearts of all.
Know him in the depths of meditation.
May he grant us immortality.

18 Know him to be the supreme source of all
Religions, ruler of the world of light,
Where there is neither day nor night,
Neither what is nor what is not, but only Shiva.
19 He is far beyond the reach of the mind.
He alone is. His glory fills all worlds.

20 He is far beyond the reach of the eye.
He alone is. May he, Shiva, reveal
Himself in the depths of meditation
And grant us immortality.

21-22 I live in fear of death, O Lord of Love;
I seek refuge at your feet. Protect me;
Protect us man and woman, cow and horse.

May the brave ones who seek you be released
From the bondage of death.

[v]

¹ To know the unity of all life leads
To deathlessness; to know not leads to death.
Both are hidden in the infinity
Of Brahman, who is beyond both.

² He is the One who presides over all
And rules over everyone from within.
He sows the golden seed of life when time begins
And helps us know its unity.

³ He is the Lord who casts the net of birth
And death and withdraws it again,
The supreme Self who governs the forces of life.

⁴ As the sun shines and fills all space with light,
Above, below, across, so shines the Lord
Of Love and fills the hearts of all created beings.

⁵ From him the cosmos comes, he who teaches
Each living creature to attain perfection
According to its own nature. He is
The Lord of Love who reigns over all life.

⁶ He is the supreme creator, hidden

Deep in the mystery of the scriptures.
By realizing him the gods and sages
Attained immortality.

7 Under the hypnotic spell of pleasure
And pain, we live for ourselves and are bound.
Though master of ourselves, we roam about
From birth to birth, driven by our own deeds.

8 The Self, small as the thumb, dwelling in the heart,
Is like the sun shining in the sky.
But when identified with the ego,
The Self appears other than what it is.
9 It may appear smaller than a hair's breadth.
But know the Self to be infinite.

10 Not female, male, nor neuter is the Self.
As is the body, so is the gender.
11 The Self takes on a body with desires,
Attachments, and delusions, and is
Born again and again in new bodies
To work out the karma of former lives.

12 The embodied self assumes many forms,
Heavy or light, according to its needs
For growth and the deeds of previous lives.
This evolution is a divine law.

13 Love the Lord and be free. He is the One
Who appears as many, enveloping
The cosmos, without beginning or end.
None but the pure in heart can realize him.

14 May Lord Shiva, creator, destroyer,
The abode of all beauty and wisdom,
Free us from the cycle of birth and death.

[V I]

1 The learned say life is self-created;
Others say life evolved from time. In truth
The Lord brought the cosmos out of himself.

2 He is pure consciousness, omnipresent,
Omnipotent, omniscient, creator
Of time and master of the three gunas.
Evolution takes place at his command.

3 Those who act without thought of personal
Profit and lead a well-disciplined life
Discover in course of time the divine
Principle that all forms of life are one.
4 They work in the service of the Lord and
Are freed from the law of karma.

5 Know him to be the primal source of life

Whose glory permeates the universe,
Who is beyond time and space, yet can be
Seen within the heart in meditation.

⁶ Know him to be beyond the tree of life,
Whose power makes all the planets revolve:
Who is both law and mercy, yet can be
Seen within the heart in meditation.

⁷ Know him to be the supreme Lord of lords,
King of kings, God of gods, ruler of all,
⁸ Without action or organs of action,
Whose power is seen in myriad ways.

⁹ Know him to be the cause without a cause,
Without a second, parent or master.
¹⁰ May he, Lord of Love, who hides himself
In his creatures like a spider in its web,
Grant us illumination.

¹¹ The Lord is hidden in the hearts of all.
The eternal witness, pure consciousness,
He watches our work from within, beyond
The reach of the gunas.

¹² The Lord is the operator; we are
But his innumerable instruments.
May we realize him in our consciousness

And find the bliss he alone can give us.

¹³ Changeless amidst the changing, consciousness
Of the conscious, he grants all our prayers.
May we realize him in our consciousness
And find the freedom he alone can give us.

¹⁴ There shines not the sun, neither moon nor star,
Nor flash of lightning, nor fire lit on earth.
Everything reflects the light of the Lord.
¹⁵ May we realize him in our consciousness;
There is no other way to conquer death.

¹⁶ He is the maker of the universe,
Self-existent, omniscient, destroyer
Of death, the source and inmost Self of all,
Ruler of the cycle of birth and death.
May we realize him in our consciousness;
There is no other way to conquer death.

¹⁷ He is the protector of the cosmos,
All glory, all-knowing, omnipresent.
How could there be any ruler but he?
May we realize him in our consciousness;
There is no other way to conquer death.

¹⁸⁻¹⁹ Lord Shiva is my refuge, he who grants
Freedom from the cycle of birth and death.

Lord Shiva is my refuge, he who gave
The sacred scriptures at the dawn of time.
Lord Shiva is my refuge, he who is
The source of purity and perfection.
Lord Shiva is my refuge, he who is
The bridge from death to immortality.
Lord Shiva is my refuge, he whose grace
Has made me long for his lotus feet.

20 How can we roll up the sky like a piece
Of deerskin? How can we end our misery
Without realizing the Lord of Love who
Is enshrined in our heart of hearts?

21 Sage Shvetashvatara realized the Lord
In meditation through infinite grace
And imparted this highest wisdom
To devoted disciples.

22 This highest mystical experience,
Revealed at the dawn of time, must be shared
Only with one whose heart is pure
Or with a disciple or one's own child.
23 If you have deep love for the Lord of Love
And for your teacher, the light of this teaching
Will shine in your heart. It will shine indeed!

O M *shanti shanti shanti*

◻ The Mundaka Upanishad

As the web issues out of the spider
And is withdrawn, as plants sprout
    from the earth,
As hair grows from the body, even so,
The sages say, this universe springs from
The deathless Self, the source of life.
    [1.7]

❶ *Modes of Knowing*

THE FAITH THAT HAS SUSTAINED Indian civilization, and that could be said to constitute the greatest gift of that civilization to the world today, is encapsulated in the four words of the Mundaka Upanishad which furnished the motto of the modern Indian nation: *Satyam eva jayate, nānritam,* "Truth alone prevails, not unreality" (III.1.6).

What the text goes on to say is equally inspiring: that there is a path to this Truth and it has been taken by saints and sages who went before us. We do not have to invent it, or go it alone.

When Gandhi took this path in modern times, he found that it opened not only to the liberation of India but to the liberation of the modern world from the prison house of its own violence. For that pregnant concept of *sat,* or *satya,* means "truth," "the Real," and "the Good." In the Upanishads these three great qualities are the same, and Gandhi verified that in his own long experience. These are his own words, in his classic account of his discoveries in *Satyagraha in South Africa*:

> The world rests upon the bedrock of satya or truth. *Asatya*,
> meaning untruth, also means non-existent, and satya or
> truth also means that which is. If untruth does not so much
> as exist, its victory is out of the question. And truth being
> that which is can never be destroyed. This is the doctrine of
> Satyagraha in a nutshell.

It is hard to imagine anything the modern world more needs to hear. We have surrounded ourselves with such a bleak picture of who we are and what the world is that unless we ourselves get on – or back on – this path pretty soon we hardly stand much chance of surviving our own culture. Only by turning away from unreality – from negativity and separateness – will we begin to see and build a world that's not only sustainable but nourishes and helps us realize our deepest longings for peace.

In the Mundaka Upanishad this pregnant phrase about truth and unreality is only one of many gems that have become treasured images of Hindu tradition: the two birds that represent the higher and lower selves within each of us (III.1.1), the river of individual existence merging into the sea of Reality (III.2.8), the seeker firing himself like an arrow into the heart of God (II.2.3), and others (see I.1.7, II.1.1, II.2.10). The Mundaka is in that sense a bit like the Bible or *Hamlet*: in reading it you keep on running across treasures of poetry and wisdom you've heard before; they have entered public domain.

Probably this is one reason why the Mundaka has been popular down the ages; no collection of the Upanishads fails to include it. Another reason is its well-balanced exposition of spiritual reality. All the major themes of the Upanishadic vision are integrated in this text: OM, prana, creation, sage and student, the nature of the Self and Brahman. The story that frames all this imagery, and the leading question of Shaunaka to the great sage Angiras that launches this Upanishad, concern appropriately the fundamental topic of truth and learning. Here once again we meet the distinction between "lower" knowledge and the "higher" knowledge that is better called realization, which draws us out of the world of appearance to a realm where knowing, being, and acting are the same.

— M . N .

O M

May we hear only what is good for all.
May we see only what is good for all.
May we serve you, Lord of Love, all our life.
May we be used to spread your peace
        on earth.

O M *shanti shanti shanti*

॥ *The Mundaka Upanishad*

PART I

[1]

¹ From infinite Godhead came forth Brahma,

First among gods, from whom sprang the cosmos.

Brahma gave the vision of the Godhead,

The true source of wisdom that life demands,

² To his eldest son, Atharva, who gave it

To Angi. In turn Angi gave it

To Satyavaha. In this tradition

Satyavaha gave it to Angiras.

³ A great householder named Shaunaka once came

To Angiras and reverently asked:

"What is that by knowing which all is known?"

⁴ He replied: "The illumined sages say

Knowledge is twofold, higher and lower.

⁵ The study of the Vedas, linguistics,

Rituals, astronomy, and all the arts

Can be called lower knowledge. The higher
Is that which leads to Self-realization.

6 "The eye cannot see it; mind cannot grasp it.
The deathless Self has neither caste nor race,
Neither eyes nor ears nor hands nor feet.
Sages say this Self is infinite in the great
And in the small, everlasting and changeless,
The source of life.

7 "As the web issues out of the spider
And is withdrawn, as plants sprout from the earth,
As hair grows from the body, even so,
The sages say, this universe springs from
The deathless Self, the source of life.

8 "The deathless Self meditated upon
Himself and projected the universe
As evolutionary energy.
From this energy developed life, mind,
The elements, and the world of karma,
Which is enchained by cause and effect.

9 "The deathless Self sees all, knows all. From him
Springs Brahma, who embodies the process
Of evolution into name and form
By which the One appears to be many."

[2]

¹ The rituals and the sacrifices described
In the Vedas deal with lower knowledge.
The sages ignored these rituals
And went in search of higher knowledge.

²⁻⁵ Look at these rituals: When the fire is lit,
Pour butter into the fire in two spots;
Then place the offering between these two.
These oblations will take the worshipper
⁶ On the sun's rays to the world of Brahma,
Where he can have his fill of enjoyment.

⁷ Such rituals are unsafe rafts for crossing
The sea of *samsara,* of birth and death.
Doomed to shipwreck are those who try to cross
The sea of samsara on these poor rafts.
⁸ Ignorant of their ignorance, yet wise
In their own esteem, these deluded men
Proud of their vain learning go round and round
Like the blind led by the blind.

⁹⁻¹⁰ Living in darkness, immature, unaware
Of any higher good or goal, they fall
Again and again into the sea.

¹¹ But those who are pure in heart, who practice
Meditation and conquer their senses

And passions, shall attain the immortal Self,
Source of all light and source of all life.

[12] Action prompted by pleasure or profit
Cannot help anyone to cross this sea.
Seek a teacher who has realized the Self.
[13] To a student whose heart is full of love,
Who has conquered his senses and passions,
The teacher will reveal the Lord of Love.

PART II

[1]

[1] Imperishable is the Lord of Love.
As from a blazing fire thousands of sparks
Leap forth, so millions of beings arise
From the Lord of Love and return to him.

[2] The Lord of Love is above name and form.
He is present in all and transcends all.
Unborn, without body and without mind,
From him comes every body and mind.
[3] He is the source of space, air, fire, water,
And the earth that holds us all.

[4] Fire is his head, the sun and moon his eyes,
The heavens his ears, the scriptures his voice,
The air his breath, the universe his heart,

And the earth his footrest. The Lord of Love
Is the innermost Self of all.

5 From him comes the fire that burns in the sun;
From the sky lit by sun and moon comes rain;
From rain comes food, from food the sexual seed;
All finally come from the Lord of Love.

6 From him come the scriptures, chants, and prayers,
Religious rites and sacrificial gifts;
From him come work, time, and givers of gifts,
And all things under the sun and moon.

7 From him come the gods of the natural world,
Men, beasts, and birds, and food to nourish them;
From him come all spiritual disciplines,
Meditation, truth, faith, and purity.

8 From him come the seven organs of sense,
Seven hot desires and their sevenfold objects,
And the seven levels of consciousness
In the cavern of the heart.

9 From him come all the seas and the mountains,
The rivers and the plants that support life.
As the innermost Self of all, he dwells
Within the cavern of the heart.

¹⁰ The Lord of Love is the one Self of all.
He is detached work, spiritual wisdom,
And immortality. Realize the Self
Hidden in the heart, and cut asunder
The knot of ignorance here and now.

[2]

¹ Bright but hidden, the Self dwells in the heart.
Everything that moves, breathes, opens, and closes
Lives in the Self. He is the source of love
And may be known through love but not through
    thought.
He is the goal of life. Attain this goal!

² The shining Self dwells hidden in the heart.
Everything in the cosmos, great and small,
Lives in the Self. He is the source of life,
Truth beyond the transience of this world.
He is the goal of life. Attain this goal!

³ Take the great bow of the sacred scriptures,
Place on it the arrow of devotion;
Then draw the bowstring of meditation
And aim at the target, the Lord of Love.
⁴ The mantram is the bow, the aspirant
Is the arrow, and the Lord the target.

Now draw the bowstring of meditation,
And hitting the target be one with him.

5 In his robe are woven heaven and earth,
Mind and body. Realize him as the One
Behind the many and stop all vain talk.
He is the bridge from death to deathless life.

6 Where all the nerves meet like spokes in a wheel,
There he dwells, the One behind the many.
Meditate upon him in the mantram.
May he guide us from death to deathless life!

7 He knows everyone and sees everything.
It is his glory that fills the cosmos.
He resides in the city of the heart.
8 It is his power that moves body and mind.
May he guide us from death to deathless life!

9 When he is seen within us and without,
He sets right all doubts and dispels the pain
Of wrong actions committed in the past.

10 In the golden city of the heart dwells
The Lord of Love, without parts, without stain.
Know him as the radiant light of lights.
11 There shines not the sun, neither moon nor star,
Nor flash of lightning, nor fire lit on earth.

The Lord is the light reflected by all.
He shining, everything shines after him.

[12] The Lord of Love is before and behind.
He extends to the right and to the left.
He extends above; he extends below.
There is no one here but the Lord of Love.
He alone is; in truth, he alone is.

PART III

[1]

[1] Like two golden birds perched on the selfsame tree,
Intimate friends, the ego and the Self
Dwell in the same body. The former eats
The sweet and sour fruits of the tree of life
While the latter looks on in detachment.

[2] As long as we think we are the ego,
We feel attached and fall into sorrow.
But realize that you are the Self, the Lord
Of life, and you will be freed from sorrow.
[3] When you realize that you are the Self,
Supreme source of light, supreme source of love,
You transcend the duality of life
And enter into the unitive state.

4 The Lord of Love shines in the hearts of all.
Seeing him in all creatures, the wise
Forget themselves in the service of all.
The Lord is their joy, the Lord is their rest;
Such as they are the lovers of the Lord.

5 By truth, meditation, and self-control
One can enter into this state of joy
And see the Self shining in a pure heart.

6 Truth is victorious, never untruth.
Truth is the way; truth is the goal of life,
Reached by sages who are free from self-will.

7 The effulgent Self, who is beyond thought,
Shines in the greatest, shines in the smallest,
Shines in the farthest, shines in the nearest,
Shines in the secret chamber of the heart.

8 Beyond the reach of the senses is he,
But not beyond the reach of a mind stilled
Through the practice of deep meditation.
9 Beyond the reach of words and works is he,
But not beyond the reach of a pure heart
Freed from the sway of the senses.

10 Sages are granted all the help they need
In everything they do to serve the Lord.

Let all those who seek their own fulfillment
Love and honor the illumined sage.

[2]

[1] The wise have attained the unitive state,
And see only the resplendent Lord of Love.
Desiring nothing in the physical world,
They have become one with the Lord of Love.

[2] Those who dwell on and long for sense-pleasure
Are born in a world of separateness.
But let them realize they are the Self
And all separateness will fall away.

[3] Not through discourse, not through the intellect,
Not even through study of the scriptures
Can the Self be realized. The Self reveals
Himself to the one who longs for the Self.
Those who long for the Self with all their heart
Are chosen by the Self as his own.

[4] Not by the weak, not by the unearnest,
Not by those who practice wrong disciplines
Can the Self be realized. The Self reveals
Himself as the Lord of Love to the one
Who practices right disciplines.

⁵ What the sages sought they have found at last.
No more questions have they to ask of life.
With self-will extinguished, they are at peace.
Seeing the Lord of Love in all around,
Serving the Lord of Love in all around,
They are united with him forever.

⁶ They have attained the summit of wisdom
By the steep path of renunciation.
They have attained to immortality
And are united with the Lord of Love.
⁷ When they leave the body, the vital force
Returns to the cosmic womb, but their work
Becomes a beneficial force in life
To bring others together in the Self.

⁸ The flowing river is lost in the sea;
The illumined sage is lost in the Self.
The flowing river has become the sea;
The illumined sage has become the Self.

⁹ Those who know the Self become the Self.
None in their family forgets the Self.
Freed from the fetters of separateness,
They attain to immortality.

¹⁰ Let this wisdom be taught only to those
Who obey the law of life's unity.

Let this wisdom be taught only to those
Who offer their lives to the Lord of Love.

[11] This is the great truth taught in ancient times
By the sage Angiras to Shaunaka.
Let us adore the illumined sages!
Let us adore the illumined sages!

OM *shanti shanti shanti*

11: *The Mandukya Upanishad*

AUM stands for the supreme Reality.
It is a symbol for what was, what is,
And what shall be. AUM represents also
What lies beyond past, present, and future.
[1]

INTRODUCTION

I: *Consciousness & Its Phases*

THE MANDUKYA IS THE BRIEFEST of the major Upanishads. Shankara declared that if one could only study a single Upanishad it should be this one, and we can see why: in its succinctness the Mandukya captures the essentials of mystical insight. One of the four Upanishadic *mahavakyas,* "great sayings" that are packed into a brief formulaic utterance, occurs in the second verse: *ayam ātmā brahma,* "the Self is Brahman." This is probably why, in a much later text, Rama tells a devotee that "the Mandukya alone is sufficient for deliverance," though less advanced seekers will have to read the ten principal Upanishads, or thirty-two, or all one hundred and eight.

The twelve verses of the Mandukya revolve around a fundamental proposition underlying the entire Vedantic worldview and mysticism generally: that one Reality (called Brahman in the Upanishads) has become the infinite variety of shifting things that we experience around us in the universe or within us as the various states of our own consciousness.

The latter field of investigation forms the first of two passes through this basic idea that make up this text. In this pass we are walked through the four states of consciousness that we all experience: the waking state, dreaming sleep, dreamless sleep, in which the autonomic nervous system rests, and finally an indescribable state of consciousness the text calls simply *turiya*, "the fourth." Like many such series in the Upanishads, these stages are steps from the everyday reality to the supreme experience. In this final state the sense of "I" is temporarily suspended. Surprisingly, the Upanishad tells us that we enter this state regularly, if we could only be aware of it: every night we are "like someone unknowingly walking back and forth over a buried treasure" (Chandogya Ⅷ.3.2). So near and yet so far.

But we have already been told, in the opening verse, that the supreme reality into which we merge in the "fourth" state is also represented by the sacred syllable AUM. So the sage takes another pass through the stages of being where the three "worlds" or orders of reality are seen in the sounds of this sacred syllable – *a*, *u*, and *m* – as it is manifested in the phenomenal world.

It is very common for an Upanishad to present us with multiple passes like this through levels of reality reminiscent of what in the Middle Ages was called the Great Chain of Being. What is different here is that the Mandukya hints that there is a way to climb that chain. AUM stands for the mantram – a form of sacred utterance, like the repetition of a name of God, used in every major spiritual tradition to still the mind and become aware of the divine Reality to which it refers. All mantrams, according to the Mandukya, go back to AUM, and then beyond even that primordial energy to Brahman, the ultimate goal of spiritual progress.

So the Upanishad first gives us an inspiring picture of "that which is," reassuring us that reality is not limited to the world of changing phenomena, and then hints at an everyday, doable way to reascend the orders of being and regain our spiritual home in the changeless. Shankara did well to praise the condensed power of this Upanishad.

– M . N .

May we hear only what is good for all.
May we see only what is good for all.
May we serve you, Lord of Love, all our life.
May we be used to spread your peace
        on earth.

O M *shanti shanti shanti*

ⅱ: *The Mandukya Upanishad*

[1] A U M stands for the supreme Reality.
It is a symbol for what was, what is,
And what shall be. A U M represents also
What lies beyond past, present, and future.

[2] Brahman is all, and the Self is Brahman.
This Self has four states of consciousness.

[3] The first is called Vaishvanara, in which
One lives with all the senses turned outward,
Aware only of the external world.

[4] Taijasa is the name of the second,
The dreaming state in which, with the senses
Turned inward, one enacts the impressions
Of past deeds and present desires.

[5] The third state is called Prajna, of deep sleep,
In which one neither dreams nor desires.
There is no mind in Prajna, there is no

Separateness; but the sleeper is not
Conscious of this. Let him become conscious
In Prajna and it will open the door
To the state of abiding joy.

6 Prajna, all-powerful and all-knowing,
Dwells in the hearts of all as the ruler.
Prajna is the source and end of all.

7 The fourth is the superconscious state called
Turiya, neither inward nor outward,
Beyond the senses and the intellect,
In which there is none other than the Lord.
He is the supreme goal of life. He is
Infinite peace and love. Realize him!

8 Turiya is represented by AUM.
Though indivisible, it has three sounds.

9 *A* stands for Vaishvanara. Those who know this,
Through mastery of the senses, obtain
The fruit of their desires and attain greatness.

10 *U* indicates Taijasa. Those who know this,
By mastering even their dreams, become
Established in wisdom. In their family
Everyone leads the spiritual life.

[11] *M* corresponds to Prajna. Those who know this,
By stilling the mind, find their true stature
And inspire everyone around to grow.

[12] The mantram A U M stands for the supreme state
Of turiya, without parts, beyond birth
And death, symbol of everlasting joy.
Those who know A U M as the Self become the Self;
Truly they become the Self.

    O M *shanti shanti shanti*

II: The Kena Upanishad

The light of Brahman flashes in lightning;
The light of Brahman flashes in our eyes.
It is the power of Brahman that makes
The mind to think, desire, and will. Therefore
Use this power to meditate on Brahman.

    [IV.4–6]

ⓘ *Who Moves the World?*

At a conference held in new Orleans some years ago, physicists were challenged to explain why there were no pioneers on the order of Einstein, Bohr, and Heisenberg any more. One young physicist pointed out that the comparison was a bit unfair. Those bold visionaries had been exploring the world outside, while his generation was faced with the infinitely harder task of querying, Who is the investigator? How is the mind, our instrument of knowing, supposed to turn around and know itself?

In India it seems that this point had been reached and crossed very early. Fundamental questions about reality are found even as early as the Rig Veda:

> What was all this before creation?
>
> Was there water?
>
> Only God knows, or perhaps he knows not . . . (x.129)

By the time we reach the Upanishads this kind of questioning is no longer speculative but has become a systematic and relentless pursuit of truth, and it embraced the realization that to know truth we have to come to grips with the medium of knowing and the identity of the knower.

This is the realization that turns mere knowing into realization, objective science into mystical awareness. There is a Sufi story about a seeker who calls on Allah day in and day out for years and finally throws himself down and sobs, "How long have I been calling and you do not answer!" Then he hears a voice: "Who do you think has been making you call me?"

Kena, the title and opening word of the present Upanishad, means "by whom?" – that is, impelled by whom do all the motions of life stir? Or in Shankara's brilliant paraphrase, "By whose mere presence does that desire arise which moves the universe?"

The text's answer is clear. The first thirteen verses declare, "He is the ear of the ear": that is, that which moves the world is consciousness, which in the human being becomes cognition, among other vital functions. Note that among the powers that operate our senses we meet "that which makes the mind think." Mind was a sense, in the Vedantic worldview, in fact, the chief sense. This is a little easier to understand when we take into account that the word we translate as "sense" is actually *indriya,* "power, faculty."

Then comes a parable. Among the gods (the faculties

of perception) only Indra has the staying power to merit instruction from the goddess of wisdom, Uma, the divine consort of Shiva. She teaches that the victory of the Vedic gods over their adversaries (the creative triumph of order over chaos) has not been theirs but that of the supreme power working through them. This is an allegory of the message which sent the Isha Upanishad so deeply into Gandhi's consciousness, about acting without attachment to the results. The victory of good over evil is guaranteed – but not by the doer. We cannot win that victory, but we can make ourselves instruments of it, precisely by not thinking of ourselves as the doers but by "making ourselves zero," in Gandhi's phrase. This is an immediate, practical consequence of the realization that we are not really the ultimate doer of any of "our" actions, including the act of knowing: "It is the power of Brahman that makes the mind to think ... Therefore, use this power to meditate on Brahman" (iv.5–6).

With an assurance that this truth is all the seeker need discover, the Kena ends.

– M . N .

Lead me from the unreal to the Real.
Lead me from darkness to light.
Lead me from death to immortality.

O M *shanti shanti shanti*

ꞏ The Kena Upanishad

[1]

THE STUDENT

1 Who makes my mind think?
Who fills my body with vitality?
Who causes my tongue to speak? Who is that
Invisible one who sees through my eyes
And hears through my ears?

THE TEACHER

2 The Self is the ear of the ear,
The eye of the eye, the mind of the mind,
The word of words, and the life of life.
Rising above the senses and the mind
And renouncing separate existence,
The wise realize the deathless Self.

3 Him our eyes cannot see, nor words express;
He cannot be grasped even by the mind.

We do not know, we cannot understand,
4 Because he is different from the known
And he is different from the unknown.
Thus have we heard from the illumined ones.

5 That which makes the tongue speak but cannot be
Spoken by the tongue, know that as the Self.
This Self is not someone other than you.

6 That which makes the mind think but cannot be
Thought by the mind, that is the Self indeed.
This Self is not someone other than you.

7 That which makes the eye see but cannot be
Seen by the eye, that is the Self indeed.
This Self is not someone other than you.

8 That which makes the ear hear but cannot be
Heard by the ear, that is the Self indeed.
This Self is not someone other than you.

9 That which makes you draw breath but cannot be
Drawn by your breath, that is the Self indeed.
This Self is not someone other than you.

[II]

THE TEACHER

¹ If you think, "I know the Self," you know not.

All you can see is his external form.

Continue, therefore, your meditation.

THE STUDENT

² I do not think I know the Self, nor can

I say I know him not.

THE TEACHER

There is only one way to know the Self,

And that is to realize him yourself.

³ The ignorant think the Self can be known

By the intellect, but the illumined

Know he is beyond the duality

Of the knower and the known.

⁴ The Self is realized in a higher state

Of consciousness when you have broken through

The wrong identification that you are

The body, subject to birth and death.

To be the Self is to go beyond death.

⁵ Realize the Self, the shining goal of life!

If you do not, there is only darkness.

See the Self in all, and go beyond death.

[III]

¹ Once upon a time the gods defeated

The demons; and though the victory

Was brought about through the power of Brahman,

The gods boasted, "Ours is the victory,

And ours the power and glory."

² Brahman saw their foolish pride and appeared

Before them. But they recognized him not.

³ They said to Agni, god of fire, "Find out

Who this mysterious being is." "I will,"

⁴ Promised Agni and approached the being.

"Who are you?" asked the mysterious one.

"I am Agni, god of fire, known to all."

⁵ "Are you powerful?" "I can burn all on earth."

⁶ "Burn this:" and Brahman placed a straw in front.

The god of fire attacked the straw, but failed

To burn it. Then he ran back to the gods

And confessed, "I have failed to discover

Who this mysterious being is."

⁷ They said to Vayu, god of air, "Find out

Who this mysterious being is." "I will,"

⁸ Promised Vayu and approached the being.

"Who are you?" asked the mysterious one.

"I am Vayu, god of air, king of space."

⁹ "Are you powerful?" "I can blow all away."

¹⁰ "Blow this away." Brahman placed a straw in front.
The god of air attacked the straw, but failed
To move it. Then he ran back to the gods
And confessed, "I have failed to discover
Who this mysterious being is."

¹¹ They begged Indra, leader of gods, "Find out
Who this mysterious being is." "I will,"
Promised Indra and approached the being,
¹² Who disappeared instantly. In his place
Appeared the lovely goddess of wisdom,
Uma, daughter of the Himalayas;
And Indra asked her, "Who was that being?"

[IV]

¹ Uma replied, "That was Brahman, from whom
Comes all your power and glory." The gods
Realized at last the Self is Brahman.
²⁻³ Agni, Vayu, Indra – these three excel
Among the gods because they realized Brahman.

⁴ The light of Brahman flashes in lightning;
The light of Brahman flashes in our eyes.
⁵ It is the power of Brahman that makes
⁶ The mind to think, desire, and will. Therefore
Use this power to meditate on Brahman.

He is the inmost Self of everyone;
He alone is worthy of all our love.
Meditate upon him in all. Those who
Meditate upon him are dear to all.

THE STUDENT
7 Teach me more of this spiritual wisdom.

THE TEACHER
I shall share with you fully what I know.
8 Meditation, control of the senses
And passions, and selfless service of all
Are the body, the scriptures are the limbs,
And truth is the heart of this wisdom.

9 Those who realize Brahman shall conquer
All evil and attain the supreme state.
Truly they shall attain the supreme state!

O M *shanti shanti shanti*

II: The Prashna Upanishad

Prana burns as fire; he shines as the sun;
He rains as the cloud; he blows as the wind;
He crashes as the thunder in the sky.
He is the earth; he has form and no form;
Prana is immortality.

    [II.5]

I: *The Breath of Life*

THE STRUCTURE OF THE PRASHNA Upanishad is quite simple: six illustrious seekers approach the sage Pippalada in turn and ask him a basic question about Reality. This allows the sage to begin with the process of creation, or the emanation of the world's innumerable forms from the divine, as many Upanishads do. Then the questions probe progressively deeper into the practical mysteries of human existence.

In his first answer Pippalada invokes the law of duality by which the One becomes many through complementary opposites like consciousness and matter, giving rise to the various orders of reality down to the sensible world in which we consciously operate. Pippalada names the primary polarity *prana* and *rayi*, roughly consciousness and matter, and his answer to the second question – "What power quickens life?" – begins with a thought-experiment on the primacy of prana over all vital functions. This becomes a hymn to prana, the distinctive theme of this Upanishad.

Prana is one of those precise but broad-ranging terms in the lexicon of Vedanta which we will say more about in the afterword. We can call it a technical term for the energy which fuels evolution, powers the vital processes in all forms of life, and ultimately becomes thoughts and desires in the mind, where it becomes most readily accessible for us to conserve or redirect. Around the concept of prana the Upanishads develop a comprehensive theory of life which accounts for everything from health to morality. Thus the questions and answers can become more penetrating, and the sweep of reality to be explained more ample, as this great concept is explored.

Answer 3 begins with the striking image (partly also at Brihadaranyaka II.1.12 and III.9.14) of the Self casting prana into the world of multiplicity as its shadow. Our real self is, of course, closer to energy or consciousness (prana) than to a form or name (rayi). Pippalada's answer goes on to categorize the five pranas known in vital functioning, with their macrocosmic equivalents (e.g., 3.8, 4.8). The Self of the Upanishads is both deeper and less circumscribed from the outside world than the usual Western conception of the self (if indeed we have one: Huston Smith has pointed out that "there is no consistent view of human nature in the West today").

Answer 4, delving deeper into the question of human identity, brings in another set of inner–outer equivalents discussed in the introduction to the Chandogya Upanishad, that of the sacrifice. Answer 5 brings in the cosmic syllable O M . And 6 closes by underscoring, if we needed further emphasis, that prana is prior to and has given rise to "name and form" (*nāma-rūpa*): in other words, to all conditioned reality. "Name and form," roughly, is the Indian equivalent of the Kantian categories of time and space, as the givens which make possible but also set limits around what the mind can grasp.

— M . N .

May we hear only what is good for all.
May we see only what is good for all.
May we serve you, Lord of Love, all our life.
May we be used to spread your peace
     on earth.

O M *shanti shanti shanti*

🔟 *The Prashna Upanishad*

QUESTION I

1 Sukesha, Satyakama, and Gargya,
Kausalya, Bhargava, and Kabandhi,
Who were all seeking Self-realization,
Approached with love sage Pippalada
For his guidance on the spiritual path.

2 The sage told them: "Live with me for one year,
Practicing sense-restraint and complete trust.
Ask me questions at the end of the year,
And I will answer them if I can."

3 After a year Kabandhi asked the sage:
"Master, who created the universe?"

4 The sage replied:
"The Lord meditated and brought forth prana
With rayi, the giver of name and form:

Male and female, so that they would bring forth
Innumerable creatures for him.

5 "Prana is the sun; rayi is the moon.
Matter is solid, matter is subtle;
Rayi therefore is present everywhere.

6–7 "The sun gives light and life to all who live,
East and west, north and south, above, below;
It is the prana of the universe.

8 "The wise see the Lord of Love in the sun,
Rising in all its golden radiance
To give its warmth and light and life to all.

9 "The wise see the Lord of Love in the year,
Which has two paths, the northern and the southern.
Those who observe outward forms of worship
And are content with personal pleasures
Travel after death by the southern path,
The path of the ancestors and of rayi,
To the lunar world, and are born again.

10 "But those who seek the Self through meditation,
Self-discipline, wisdom, and faith in God
Travel after death by the northern path,
The path of prana, to the solar world,

Supreme refuge, beyond the reach of fear
And free from the cycle of birth and death.

11 "Some look upon the sun as our father
Who makes life possible with heat and rain
And divides time into months and seasons.
Others have seen him riding in wisdom
On his chariot, with seven colors
As horses and six wheels to represent
The whirling spokes of time.

12 "The wise see the Lord of Love in the month;
Rayi is the dark half, prana the bright.
The wise worship in the light of wisdom,
Others in the darkness of ignorance.

13 "The wise see the Lord of Love in the day;
Rayi is the dark night, prana daylight.
Those who use their days for sexual pleasure
Consume prana, the very stuff of life;
But mastered, sex becomes a spiritual force.

14 "The wise see the Lord of Love in all food;
From food comes seed, and from seed all creatures.
15 They take the lunar path who live for sex;
But those who are self-controlled and truthful
Will go to the bright regions of the sun.

[16] "The bright world of Brahman can be attained
Only by those who are pure and true,
Only by those who are pure and true."

QUESTION II

[1] Then Bhargava approached the sage and asked:
"Master, what powers support this body?
Which of them are manifested in it?
And among them all, which is the greatest?"

[2] The sage replied: "The powers are space, air, fire,
Water, earth, speech, mind, vision, and hearing.
All these boasted, 'We support this body.'
[3] But prana, vital energy, supreme
Over them all, said, 'Don't deceive yourselves.
It is I, dividing myself fourfold,
Who hold this body together.'

[4] "But they would not believe these words of prana.
To demonstrate the truth, prana arose
And left the body, and all the powers
Knew they had to leave as well. When prana
Returned to the body, they too were back.
As when the queen bee goes out, all the bees
Go out, and when she returns all return,
So returned speech, mind, vision, and hearing.
Then the powers understood and sang this song:

⁵ 'Prana burns as fire; he shines as the sun;

He rains as the cloud; he blows as the wind;

He crashes as the thunder in the sky.

He is the earth; he has form and no form;

Prana is immortality.

⁶ 'Everything rests in prana, as spokes rest

In the hub of the wheel: all the Vedas,

All the rituals, all the warriors and kings.

⁷ 'O prana, you move in the mother's womb

As life to be manifested again.

All creatures pay their homage to you.

⁸ 'You carry offerings to gods and ancestors

And help sages to master their senses,

Which depend upon you for their function.

⁹ 'You are the creator and destroyer,

And our protector. You shine as the sun

In the sky; you are the source of all light.

¹⁰ 'When you pour yourself down as rain on earth,

Every living creature is filled with joy

And knows food will be abundant for all.

¹¹ 'You are pure and master of everything.

As fire you receive our oblations;

It is you who gives us the breath of life.

¹² 'Be kind to us with your invisible form,
Which dwells in the voice, the eye, and the ear,
And pervades the mind. Abandon us not.

¹³ 'O prana, all the world depends on you.
As a mother looks after her children,
Look after us. Grant us wealth and wisdom.'"

QUESTION III

¹ Then Kausalya approached the sage and asked:
"Master, from what source does this prana come?
How does he enter the body, how live
After dividing himself into five,
How leave the body at the time of death?
How does he support all that is without
And all that is within?"

² The sage replied: "You ask searching questions.
Since you are a devoted aspirant
Seeking Brahman, I shall answer them.

³ "Prana is born of the Self. As a man
Casts a shadow, the Self casts prana
Into the body at the time of birth
So that the mind's desires may be fulfilled.

⁴ "As a king appoints officers
To do his work in all the villages,

So prana works with four other pranas,
Each a part of himself, to carry out
Different functions in the body.

5 "The main prana dwells in eye, ear, mouth, and nose;
Apana, the downward force, in the organs
Of sex and of excretion. Samana,
The equalizing force in the middle,
Digests food and kindles the seven fires.

6 "Vyana, distributor of energy,
Moves through the myriad vital currents
Radiating from the heart, where lives the Self.
7 At the time of death, through the subtle track
That runs upward through the spinal channel,
Udana, the fifth force, leads the selfless
Up the long ladder of evolution,
And the selfish down. But those who are both
Selfless and selfish come back to this earth.

8 "The sun is the prana of the universe,
And it rises to bring light to our eyes.
The earth draws the lower fire of apana;
The space between sun and earth is samana,
And the moving air is vyana.

9 "Fire is udana. When that fire goes out,
The senses are drawn back into the mind

And the person is ready for rebirth.

10 Whatever the content of consciousness
At the time of death, that is what unites us
To prana, udana, and the Self,
To be reborn in the plane we have earned.

11 "Those who realize this go beyond death.
Their children too follow in their footsteps.
12 Those who perceive how prana rises,
Enters the body, and becomes fivefold
To serve the Self, they die not; they die not."

QUESTION IV

1 Then Gargya approached the sage and asked him:
"Sir, when a man is sleeping, who is it
That sleeps in him? Who sees the dreams he sees?
When he wakes up, who in him is awake?
When he enjoys, who is enjoying?
In whom do all these faculties rest?"

2 The sage replied: "As the rays of the sun,
When night comes, become all one in his disk
Until they spread out again at sunrise,
Even so the senses are gathered up
In the mind, which is master of them all.

Therefore when a person neither hears, sees, smells,
Tastes, touches, speaks, nor enjoys, we say he sleeps.

³ "Only the fires of prana are burning.
Apana is like the holy hearth-fire
Ever burning in the householder's shrine;
Vyana is like the fire that faces south
For carrying offerings to our ancestors;
And prana is the fire that faces eastward.
⁴ Samana is the equalizing fire
That balances inward and outward breath,
The offerings made by the mind.
Udana is the fruit of dreamless sleep,
In which the mind is led close to the Self.

⁵ "The dreaming mind recalls past impressions.
It sees again what has been seen; it hears
Again what has been heard, enjoys again
What has been enjoyed in many places.
Seen and unseen, heard and unheard, enjoyed
And unenjoyed, the real and the unreal,
The mind sees all; the mind sees all.

⁶ "When the mind is stilled in dreamless sleep,
It brings rest and repose to the body.
⁷ Just as birds fly to the tree for rest,
All things in life find their rest in the Self.

⁸ Earth, water, fire, air, space, and their subtle

Elements, the eyes and what can be seen,

The ears and what can be heard, the nostrils

And what can be smelled, the palate and what

Can be tasted, the skin and what can be touched,

The tongue and what can be spoken,

The hands and what can be held, the organ

Of sex and its object of enjoyment,

The organ of excretion and what is

Excreted, the feet and what they walk on,

The mind and what it thinks, the intellect

And what it knows, the ego and what

It grasps, the heart and what it loves, the light

And what it reveals: all things in life

Find their rest in the Self in dreamless sleep."

⁹ "It is the Self who sees, hears, smells, touches,

And tastes, who thinks, acts, and is pure
    consciousness.

The Self is Brahman, changeless and supreme."

¹⁰ "Those who know the supreme Self as formless,

Without shadow, without impurity,

Know all, gentle friend, and live in all.

¹¹ Those who know the Self, the seat of consciousness,

In whom the breath and all the senses live,

Know all, gentle friend, and live in all."

QUESTION V

¹ Satyakama approached the sage and asked:
"Those who have become established in AUM,
What happens to them after death?"

² The sage replied: "AUM is both immanent
And transcendent. Through it one can attain
The personal and the impersonal."

³ "AUM has three sounds. Those who meditate on *a*
Come back to earth, led by the Rig Veda,
To lead a pure life, full of faith and love.
⁴ Those who meditate on the first two sounds,
A and *u*, led by the Yajur Veda,
Go to the lunar world, full of pleasure,
From which they come back cloyed to earth again.
⁵ But those who meditate on *a*, *u*, and *m*
Are led by the Sama chants to the sun,
Where freed from sin, as a snake sheds its skin,
They see the supreme Lord, who lives in all."

⁶ "These three sounds when they are separated
Cannot lead one beyond mortality;
But when the whole mantram, *a*, *u*, and *m*,
Indivisible, interdependent,
Goes on reverberating in the mind,
One is freed from fear, awake or asleep.

⁷ "The Rig Veda brings one to earth; the Yajur
Escorts one to the region of the moon;
The Sama leads one to the solar world,
To which the sage attains through the mantram.
Established in this cosmic vibration,
The sage goes beyond fear, decay, and death
To enter into infinite peace."

QUESTION VI

¹ Then Sukesha approached the sage and said:
"Master, the prince of Kosala asked me
This question once: 'Sukesha, do you know the Self
With his sixteen forms?' 'I don't,' I replied.
'If I did, I would certainly tell you;
For he who speaks an untruth perishes
Like a tree without roots.' The prince mounted
His chariot and went away silent.
Now may I ask you, where is that Self?"
² The sage replied: "Within this body dwells
The Self with his sixteen forms, gentle friend.
³ The Self asked himself, 'What is it that makes
Me go if it goes and stay if it stays?'
⁴ So he created prana, and from it
Desire; and from desire he made space, air,
Fire, water, the earth, the senses, the mind,

And food; from food came strength, austerity,
The scriptures, sacrifice, and all the worlds;
And everything was given name and form.

5 "As rivers lose their private name and form
When they reach the sea, so that people speak
Of the sea alone, so all these sixteen
Forms disappear when the Self is realized.
Then there is no more name and form for us,
And we attain immortality.

6 "The Self is the hub of the wheel of life,
And the sixteen forms are only the spokes.
The Self is the paramount goal of life.
Attain this goal and go beyond death!"

7 The sage concluded: "There is nothing more
To be said of the Self, nothing more."

8 The students adored their teacher and said:
"You are our father; you have taken us
Across the sea to the other shore."
Let us adore the illumined sages!
Let us adore the illumined sages!

O M *shanti shanti shanti*

🔟 *The Taittiriya Upanishad*

The Self is the source of abiding joy.
Our hearts are filled with joy in seeing him
Enshrined in the depths of our consciousness.
If he were not there, who would breathe,
    who live?
He it is who fills every heart with joy.

   [II.7.1]

INTRODUCTION

◳ *Ascent to Joy*

THE UPANISHADS MAKE A CAREFUL distinction between the terms *pleasure* and *joy*. Pleasure, which mainly comes from sense experience, is transitory and actually quite limited. Joy comes from being in harmony with the creative forces of the universe, with one's own destiny, and is permanent – one of the main reasons we can tell it apart from pleasure – and has no limits at all. This is an important distinction in mysticism, and in a striking passage, the Taittiriya Upanishad builds on this idea and tries to give us some sense of the magnitude of the joy that is our legacy, building up systematically, in expansions of a hundred, a comparison with the limited experience that we have now to the inexpressible joy of unity with the supreme.

That alone would be an outstanding contribution, but the Taittiriya has other distinctive features. One is the model of the human being as the Self encased in five wrappings like a Chinese puzzle, starting from the material body (the first self we are generally aware of) and progressing inward to the "sheaths" of vitality (*prana*), mind, intuition (*buddhi*), and finally joy. Along with the quantum leaps in joy are similar qualitative steps in awareness for those who push deeper through these layers of condensation, as it were, that cover our real Self.

How is this to be done? Here the text gives one of those practical insights that startle us with their contemporary bearing: "Respect food . . . Waste not food . . . The earth can yield much more. . . . Refuse not food to those who are hungry." (III.8–10). Passages like these should give final proof that the religion of the Upanishads is not world-denying. The layered models that they develop in so many forms make us feel more respect for the things of this world. Food, for example, is life-energy, or prana, condensed into matter. When we respect that energy on the physical level, we gain easier passage to the level beyond. Of course, this is even more true of our fellow creatures; alienation from them blocks spiritual growth. By realizing the unity from which each created thing has come and in which it is sustained, we can live rightly in the world of change in order to ascend through it to the eternal.

Section I.11 is a famous passage in this same spirit, a kind of "convocation address" to spiritual students who have finished their course of study, the phase of life called *brahmacharya* (see p. 250); it follows naturally on section 9, here titled "To the Householder." The Upanishads are intended not only for renunciates in Himalayan caves or forest solitude; they are also very much for those who wish to carry out the dharmas of social life in the world.

Like the Kena, this Upanishad ends rather than begins with a narrative. The story of Bhrigu addresses how we can make our own life part of the upward drive of spiritual evolution by "serving the Self" in everything we do. Than that, the Upanishad asserts, there can be no greater joy.

— M . N .

May the Lord of day grant us peace.
May the Lord of night grant us peace.
May the Lord of sight grant us peace.
May the Lord of might grant us peace.
May the Lord of speech grant us peace.
May the Lord of space grant us peace.
I bow down to Brahman, source of all power.
I will speak the truth and follow the law.
Guard me and my teacher against all harm.
Guard me and my teacher against all harm.

OM *shanti shanti shanti*

II: *The Taittiriya Upanishad*

PART I

[1]

¹ May the Lord of day grant us peace.

May the Lord of night grant us peace.

May the Lord of sight grant us peace.

May the Lord of might grant us peace.

May the Lord of speech grant us peace.

May the Lord of space grant us peace.

I bow down to Brahman, source of all power.

I will speak the truth and follow the law.

Guard me and my teacher against all harm.

Guard me and my teacher against all harm.

[2]

² Let us learn the art of recitation,

Which calls for knowledge of letters, accent,

Measure, emphasis, sequence, and rhythm.

[3]

¹ May the light of wisdom illumine us.
May we become united with the Lord.
Let us contemplate five categories:
This world and luminous worlds in the sky,
Education, progeny, and speech.
What is this world? Earth below, sky above,
Air between, and space connecting them.
² What are the luminous worlds in the sky?
Fire on one side and sun on the other,
Water between, lightning connecting them.
³ What is education? Teacher speaking
To the disciple seated by his side,
Wisdom between, discourse connecting them.
⁴ What is progeny? Mother on one side,
Father on the other, the child between,
The sexual organ connecting them.

⁵ What is speech? The lower jaw and the upper,
Words between, and the tongue connecting them.
⁶ Those who contemplate these categories
Will have children, cattle, food, and wisdom.

[4]

¹ O Lord of Love, revealed in the scriptures,
Who have assumed the forms of all creatures,
Grant me wisdom to choose the path

That can lead me to immortality.

May my body be strong, my tongue be sweet;

May my ears hear always the sound of OM,

The supreme symbol of the Lord of Love,

And may my love for him grow more and more.

² Lord, may I grow in spiritual wisdom,

And may I have food and clothes and cattle.

May students come to me from far and near,

Like a flowing river all the year;

May I be enabled to guide them all

To train their senses and still their minds;

³ May this be my wealth, may this be my fame.

O Lord of Love, may I enter into you,

And may you reveal yourself unto me,

The pure One masquerading as many.

You are the refuge of all devotees.

I am your devotee. Make me your own.

[5]

¹ *Bhur*, *bhuvas*, *suvar* are three vibrations.

Mahachamasya taught a fourth, *maha*,

To stand for the Self. The rest are his limbs.

When *bhur* is the earth, *bhuvas* space between,

And *suvar* the world above, *maha* is the sun

That nourishes life everywhere.

² When *bhur* is fire, *bhuvas* air, and *suvar*

The sun, *maha* is the moon that supports

All the planets and celestial bodies.

³ When *bhur* is the Rig, *bhuvas* the Sama,

And *suvar* the Yajur, *maha* is Brahman,

Wisdom that nourishes all the four Vedas.

⁴ When *bhur* is prana upward, *bhuvas*

Downward, and *suvar* is prana widespread,

Maha is food that nourishes vital forces

In everyone. ⁵ Thus these vibrations

Are four times four. Those who understand them

Realize the Self and are loved by all.

[6]

¹ The Lord of Love dwells in the hearts of all.

To realize him is to go beyond death.

Between the parietal bones of the skull

Swings the sagittal door, as the lobe swings

Behind the palate. Through that one goes out

Chanting *bhur*, to become one with fire;

Chanting *bhuvas*, to become one with air;

Chanting *suvar*, to be one with the sun;

Chanting *maha*, to be one with the Lord.

Thus one becomes king of his own life, ruler

Of his passions, senses, and intellect.

He is united with the Lord of Love,
Who is truth, peace, and immortality,
The source of joy, the supreme goal of life.
Meditate always on the Lord of Love.

[7]

¹ Earth, sky, worlds above, quarters and their halves;
Fire, air, sun, moon, and stars; water, herbs, trees,
Space, and entity are the elements.
Eye, ear, mind, tongue, and touch; skin, flesh, muscle,
Marrow, and skeleton; and the five
Vital forces constitute the body.
The sage, contemplating these sets of five,
Discovered that everything is holy.
Man can complete the inner with the outer.

[8]

¹ OM is the supreme symbol of the Lord.
OM is the whole. OM affirms; OM signals
The chanting of the hymns from the Vedas.
The priest begins with OM; spiritual teachers
And their students commence with OM.
The student who is established in OM
Becomes united with the Lord of Love.

[9]

To the Householder

¹ Practice right conduct, learning and teaching;
Be truthful always, learning and teaching;
Master the passions, learning and teaching;
Control the senses, learning and teaching;
Strive for peace always, learning and teaching;
Rouse kundalini, learning and teaching;
Serve humanity, learning and teaching;
Beget progeny, learning and teaching.
Satyavacha says: "Be truthful always."
Taponitya says: "Master the passions."
Naka declares: "Learning and teaching are
Necessary for spiritual progress."

[10]

¹ "I have become one with the tree of life.
My glory rises like the mountain peak.
I have realized the Self, who is ever
Pure, all-knowing, radiant, and immortal."
Thus spoke sage Trishanku when he became
United with the Lord of Love.

[11]

¹ Having taught the Vedas, the teacher says:
"Speak the truth. Do your duty. Neglect not
The scriptures. Give your best to your teacher.

Do not cut off the line of progeny. Swerve not
From the truth. Swerve not from the good.
Protect your spiritual progress always.
Give your best in learning and teaching.
Never fail in respect to the sages.
[2] See the divine in your mother, father,
Teacher, and guest. Never do what is wrong.
[3] Honor those who are worthy of honor.
Give with faith. Give with love. Give with joy.
[4-5] If you are in doubt about right conduct,
Follow the example of the sages,
Who know what is best for spiritual growth.
[6] This is the instruction of the Vedas;
This is the secret; this is the message."

PART II

[1.1] They have attained the goal who realize
Brahman as the supreme reality,
The source of truth, wisdom, and boundless joy.
They see the Lord in the cave of the heart
And are granted all the blessings of life.

From Brahman came space; from space, air;
From air, fire; from fire, water; from water,
Earth; from earth, plants; from plants, food;
      and from food,

The human body, head, arms, legs, and heart.

²·¹ From food are made all bodies, which become
Food again for others after their death.
Food is the most important of all things
For the body; therefore it is the best
Medicine for all the body's ailments.
They who look upon food as the Lord's gift
Shall never lack life's physical comforts.
From food are made all bodies. All bodies
Feed on food, and it feeds on all bodies.

The physical sheath is made up of food.
Within it is contained the vital sheath,
Which has the same form, with prana as head,
Vyana as right arm, apana as left,
Space as heart, and earth as foundation.

³·¹ Man and woman, beast and bird live by breath.
Breath is therefore called the true sign of life.
It is the vital force in everyone
That determines how long we are to live.
Those who look upon breath as the Lord's gift
Shall live to complete the full span of life.

The vital sheath is made of living breath.
Within it is contained the mental sheath,
Which has the same form, with Yajur as head,

Rig as right arm, Sama as left. The heart
Is the wisdom of the Upanishads,
And the Atharva is the foundation.

4.1 Realizing That from which all words turn back
And thoughts can never reach, one knows
The bliss of Brahman and fears no more.

Within the mental sheath, made up of waves
Of thought, there is contained the sheath of wisdom.
It has the same form, with faith as the head,
Righteousness as right arm and truth as left.
Practice of meditation is its heart,
And discrimination its foundation.
5.1 Wisdom means a life of selfless service.
Even the gods seek spiritual wisdom.
Those who attain wisdom are freed from sin,
And find all their selfless desires granted.

The wisdom sheath is made of detachment.
Within it is contained the sheath of bliss,
Which has the same form, with joy as the head,
Contentment as right arm, and delight the left.
Bliss is the heart, and Brahman the foundation.
6.1 Those who deny the Lord deny themselves;
Those who affirm the Lord affirm themselves.
The wise, not the unwise, realize the Lord.

The Lord of Love willed: "Let me be many!"
And in the depths of his meditation
He created everything that exists.
Meditating, he entered into everything.

He who has no form assumed many forms;
He who is infinite appeared finite;
He who is everywhere assumed a place;
He who is all wisdom caused ignorance;
He who is real caused unreality.
It is he who has become everything.
It is he who gives reality to all.
[7.1] Before the universe was created,
Brahman existed as unmanifest.
Brahman brought the Lord out of himself;
Therefore he is called the Self-existent.

The Self is the source of abiding joy.
Our hearts are filled with joy in seeing him
Enshrined in the depths of our consciousness.
If he were not there, who would breathe, who live?
He it is who fills every heart with joy.

When one realizes the Self, in whom
All life is one, changeless, nameless, formless,
Then one fears no more. Until we realize
The unity of life, we live in fear.

For the mere scholar who knows not the Self,

His separateness becomes fear itself.

8.1 Through fear of Brahman the wind blows,

    sun shines,

Fire burns, rain falls, and death snatches all away.

What is the joy of realizing the Self?

Take a young man, healthy, strong, good, and cultured,

Who has all the wealth that earth can offer;

Let us take this as one measure of joy.

One hundred times that joy is one measure

Of the gandharvas' joy; but no less joy

Has one illumined, free from self-will.

One hundred times that joy is one measure

Of the joy of *pitris*; but no less joy

Has one illumined, free from self-will.

One hundred times that joy is one measure

Of the joy of devas; but no less joy

Has one illumined, free from self-will.

One hundred times that joy is one measure

Of the *karmadevas'* joy; but no less joy

Has one illumined, free from self-will.

One hundred times that joy is one measure

Of the joy of Indra; but no less joy

Has one illumined, free from self-will.

One hundred times that joy is one measure

Of Brihaspati's joy; but no less joy
Has one illumined, free from self-will.
One hundred times that joy is one measure
Of the joy of Virat; but no less joy
Has one illumined, free from self-will.
One hundred times that joy is one measure
Of Prajapati's joy; but no less joy
Has one illumined, free from self-will.

The Self in man and in the sun are one.
Those who understand this see through the world
And go beyond the various sheaths of being
To realize the unity of life.

9.1 Realizing That from which all words turn back
And thoughts can never reach, they know
The bliss of Brahman and fear no more.
No more are they oppressed by the question,
"How did I fail to perform what is right?
And how did I perform what is not right?"
Those who realize the joy of Brahman,
Having known what is right and what is wrong,
Are delivered forever from this duality.

PART III

1.1 Bhrigu went to his father, Varuna,
and asked respectfully: "What is Brahman?"

Varuna replied: "First learn about food,
Breath, eye, ear, speech, and mind; then seek to know
That from which these are born, by which they live,
For which they search, and to which they return.
That is Brahman."

2.1 Bhrigu meditated and found that food
Is Brahman. From food are born all creatures,
By food they grow, and to food they return.
Not fully satisfied with his knowledge,
Bhrigu went to his father, Varuna,
And appealed: "Please teach me more of Brahman."

"Seek it through meditation," replied Varuna,
"For meditation is Brahman."

3.1 Bhrigu meditated and found that life
Is Brahman. From life are born all creatures,
By life they grow, and to life they return.
Not fully satisfied with his knowledge,
Bhrigu went to his father, Varuna,
And appealed: "Please teach me more of Brahman."

"Seek it through meditation," replied Varuna,
"For meditation is Brahman."

4.1 Bhrigu meditated and found that mind
Is Brahman. From mind are born all creatures,
By mind they grow, and to mind they return.
Not fully satisfied with his knowledge,
Bhrigu went to his father, Varuna,
And appealed: "Please teach me more of Brahman."

"Seek it through meditation," replied Varuna,
"For meditation is Brahman."

5.1 Bhrigu meditated and found that wisdom
Is Brahman. From wisdom come all creatures,
By wisdom they grow, to wisdom return.
Not fully satisfied with his knowledge,
Bhrigu went to his father, Varuna,
And appealed: "Please teach me more of Brahman."

"Seek it through meditation," replied Varuna,
"For meditation is Brahman."

6.1 Bhrigu meditated and found that joy
Is Brahman. From joy are born all creatures,
By joy they grow, and to joy they return.

Bhrigu, Varuna's son, realized this Self
In the very depths of meditation.

Those who realize the Self within the heart
Stand firm, grow rich, gather a family
Around them, and receive the love of all.

7.1 Respect food: the body is made of food;
Food and body exist to serve the Self.
Those who realize the Self within the heart
Stand firm, grow rich, gather a family
Around them, and receive the love of all.

8.1 Waste not food, waste not water, waste not fire;
Fire and water exist to serve the Self.
Those who realize the Self within the heart
Stand firm, grow rich, gather a family
Around them, and receive the love of all.

9.1 Increase food. The earth can yield much more.
Earth and space exist to serve the Self.
Those who realize the Self within the heart
Stand firm, grow rich, gather a family
Around them, and receive the love of all.

10.1 Refuse not food to those who are hungry.
When you feed the hungry, you serve the Lord,
From whom is born every living creature.
Those who realize the Self within the heart
Stand firm, grow rich, gather a family
Around them, and receive the love of all.

10.2 Realizing this makes our words pleasing,
Our breathing deep, our arms ready to serve
The Lord in all around, our feet ready
To go to the help of everyone in need.
10.3–4 Realizing this we see the Lord of Love
In beast and bird, in starlight and in joy,
In sex energy and in the grateful rain,
In everything the universe contains.
Drawing on the Lord's resources within,
Security, wisdom, and love in action,
We conquer every enemy within
To be united with the Lord of Love.

The Self in man and in the sun are one.
10.5 Those who understand this see through the world
And go beyond the various sheaths
Of being to realize the unity of life.
Those who realize that all life is one
Are at home everywhere and see themselves
In all beings. They sing in wonder:
"I am the food of life, I am, I am;
I eat the food of life, I eat, I eat.
I link food and water, I link, I link.
I am the first-born in the universe;
Older than the gods, I am immortal.
Who shares food with the hungry protects me;

Who shares not with them is consumed by me.
I am this world and I consume this world.
They who understand this understand life."

This is the Upanishad, the secret teaching.

O M *shanti shanti shanti*

Ⅱ: The Aitareya Upanishad

The Self is in all.
He is all the gods, the five elements,
Earth, air, fire, water, and space;
    all creatures,
Great or small, born of eggs, of wombs,
    of heat,
Of shoots, horses, cows, elephants, men,
    and women;
All beings that walk, all beings that fly,
And all that neither walk nor fly. .

    [III.1.3]

INTRODUCTION

0: *The Unity of Life*

PERHAPS THE GREATEST CONTRIBU-
tion of the Upanishads is to open our eyes to what it really
means to be a human being. The constant concern of the
sages is to reawaken us to the sacred nature of the environment, of living creatures, of one another, and finally of our
own inner reality. This exalted vision of the human person has
been echoed by the anonymous monk of fourteenth-century
England who has left us one of the world's greatest mystical
documents, the *Cloud of Unknowing*:

> Beneath you and external to you lies the entire created uni-
> verse. Yes, even the sun, the moon, and the stars. They are
> fixed above you, splendid in the firmament, yet they cannot
> be compared to your exalted dignity as a human being. . . .
> There is nothing above you in nature except God himself.

How can this be? How can this miniscule, fragile body
whose size in the Universe is beyond ludicrous be, or contain, such importance? Because, the Upanishads and all the
world's great mystics insist, we are not that fragile body but

that which causes it to move, breathe, and be alive: consciousness. In this Upanishad we have one of the four *mahavakyas* or "great utterances" that later tradition teased out as the sum and substance of their teaching: *prajñam brahma*, "All reality is consciousness." And the same consciousness is the life of all: thus we have the explanation for both the sanctity and the unity of life.

The Aitareya lays out this explanation by telling the story of evolution in the form of a creation myth. To us today it seems very Lamarckian because it sees the driving force of evolution as desire; but if we bear in mind that the sages understood desire to be precisely that – a force, rather than simply cravings or emotions – the myth is not so implausible. The titanic energy of evolution suggests some kind of drive; when the sages (or the early Greek thinkers) called it "desire," they were connecting life in the here-and-now to that awesome cosmic process by which the One manifested itself as, and still sustains, the many.

A great sage of modern India who was most Upanishadic in his exalted vision of this process, Sri Ramana Maharshi, replied to the urgent questions of a distinguished philosopher in words that always haunt me:

> Happiness is the very nature of the Self; happiness and the
> Self are not different. There is no happiness in any object
> of the world. We imagine through our ignorance that we
> derive happiness from objects. When the mind goes out, it

experiences misery. In truth, when its desires are fulfilled, it returns to its own place and enjoys the happiness that is the Self.

– M . N .

May my word be one with my thought,
     and my thought
Be one with my word. O Lord of Love,
Let me realize you in my consciousness.
May I realize the truth of the scriptures
And translate it into my daily life.
May I proclaim the truth of the scriptures.
May I speak the truth. May it protect me,
And may it protect my teacher.

O M *shanti shanti shanti*

II: *The Aitareya Upanishad*

PART I

[1]

1 Before the world was created, the Self
Alone existed; nothing whatever stirred.
Then the Self thought: "Let me create the world."
2 He brought forth all the worlds out of himself:
Ambhas, high above the sky; Marichi,
The sky; Mara, the middle region that is earth;
And Apa, the realm of waters below.

3 The Self thought: "I have created these worlds.
Let me now create guardians for these worlds."
From the waters he drew forth Purusha
And gave him a form. 4 As the Self brooded
Over the form, a mouth opened, as does
An egg, giving forth speech and fire; nostrils
Opened with the power of breathing the air;
Eyes opened, giving rise to sight and sun;

And ears opened to hear the sound in space.
Skin appeared and from it hair; from hair came
Plants and trees. The heart gushed forth;

    from the heart

Came the mind, and from the mind came the moon.
The navel opened with the downward force,
Apana, which gave rise to death. The sex organ rose
With living water which gave rise to birth.

[2]

¹ Thus came these guardians into the mighty
Ocean of existence. The Self caused them
To hunger and thirst. They said to the Self:
"Give us a place where we can live and eat."
² He brought them the form of a cow. They said:
"This is not what we desire." He brought them
The form of a horse. But they said again:
³ "This is not what we desire." He brought them
A human form. They said in joy: "Just right!
A human body is just right for us."
The Self asked them to enter the body
And take up their places. ⁴ Fire, becoming
Speech, entered the mouth; air, becoming smell,
Entered the nose; the sun, becoming sight,
Entered the eyes; sounds in space, becoming
Hearing, entered the ears; plants, herbs, and trees,

Becoming hair, entered the skin; the moon,
Becoming mind, entered the heart. The god
Of death, becoming downward force, entered
The navel; the god of living water,
Becoming sperm, entered the sex organ.
⁵ Hunger and thirst said to the Self: "Give us
A place." He told them: "Enter into these
Guardians and share their life with them."
Thus hunger and thirst for food, drink, and pleasure
Attend us, whatever we do in life.

[3]

¹ The Self, Creator, thought: "Here are the worlds
And their guardians. Let me now bring forth food
For them." ² He brooded over the waters,
And food appeared in the form of matter.
³ It tried to run away in fear, and man,
The first embodied being, tried to catch
It with his speech. But he could not catch it
With words. Merely by repeating the name
Of food one cannot satisfy hunger.
⁴ He tried to catch it with his breath, but he
Could not. Just by smelling food one cannot
Satisfy hunger. ⁵ He tried to catch it
With his eyes, but he could not. By looking
At food one cannot satisfy hunger.

⁶ He tried to catch it with his ears, but he
Could not. By merely hearing about food
One cannot satisfy hunger. ⁷ He tried
To catch it with his skin, but he could not.
By touching food one cannot satisfy
Hunger. ⁸ He tried to catch it with his mind,
But he could not. By thinking about food
One cannot satisfy hunger. ⁹ He tried
To catch it with his genital organ,
But he could not. By sexual union
One cannot satisfy hunger. ¹⁰ He tried
To catch it with apana, the downward prana
Of digestion, and at last he caught it.
Thus it is apana that takes in food;
Thus it is apana that lives on food.

¹¹ The Self thought, "How can this be without me?
If speaking is done by speech, breathing by
Breath, seeing by eyes, hearing by ears, smelling
By nose, and meditation by the mind,
¹² Then who am I?" Entering the body
Through the gateway at the crown of the head,
He passed into the three states of consciousness
In which the Self resides.

¹³ Filled with wonder, we sing: "I see the Lord."
¹⁴ So his name is Idamdra, "He who sees."

The name Indra stands for Idamdra.
The gods do like to sit behind a veil;
Indeed they like to sit behind a veil.

PART II
[1]
¹ Life begins in man as sexual fluid,
Which has the strength gathered from all his limbs.
Man holds this quintessence in his body,
And it becomes child in woman. This is
The first birth. ² Child and mother are one.
She protects the child, and needs protection.
³ The mother carries the child in her womb,
And the father bestows his loving care
Before and after birth. The child is their
Atman, their very Self, and continues
Their line without break as the second birth.
⁴ He discharges all their holy duties
And sheds his body, too, when it grows old,
To be born again. This is the third birth.

The sage Vamadeva declared of old:
⁵ "While dwelling in the womb I understood
The birth of all the gods. A hundred forms,
Strong as steel, held me prisoner. But I
Broke loose from them, like a hawk from the cage,

And came out swiftly." While still in the womb,
Vamadeva made this declaration.
⁶ He emerged from his mother's womb, fully
Illumined, to live in abiding joy,
And went beyond death. Indeed
He went beyond death.

PART III
[1]

¹ Who is this Self on whom we meditate?
Is it the Self by which we see, hear, smell, and taste,
² Through which we speak in words? Is Self the mind
By which we perceive, direct, understand,
Know, remember, think, will, desire, and love?
These are but servants of the Self, who is
Pure consciousness.
This Self is all in all.
He is all the gods, the five elements,
³ Earth, air, fire, water, and space; all creatures,
Great or small, born of eggs, of wombs, of heat,
Of shoots; horses, cows, elephants, men, and women;
All beings that walk, all beings that fly,
And all that neither walk nor fly. Prajna
Is pure consciousness, guiding all. The world
Rests on prajna, and prajna is Brahman.

⁴ Those who realize Brahman live in joy
And go beyond death. Indeed
They go beyond death.

OM *shanti shanti shanti*

Ⅱ *Four Minor Upanishads*

The supreme Self is neither born nor dies.
He cannot be burned, moved, pierced, cut,
    nor dried.
Beyond all attributes, the supreme Self
Is the eternal witness, ever pure,
Indivisible, and uncompounded,
Far beyond the senses and the ego.
In him conflicts and expectations cease.

    [ATMA III]

◧ *Beads of Wisdom*

A "MINOR" UPANISHAD, BY DEFINI-
tion, is one that has not been commented upon or extensively
cited by Shankara, not necessarily one that is minor in wisdom or expressive power. Shankara's commentaries elevated
the principal Upanishads into a kind of canon; but it should
be noted that the list is not fixed – various authorities, ancient
and modern, have reshaped it – and there may in any case
have been other commentaries of Shankara which have not
survived. Some of the so-called minor texts convey insights
of the same magnitude as those singled out by Shankara, usually in much the same style and often with the same force.

The first of the four minor Upanishads in this collection,
the Tejobindu, stresses the "beyondness" of Reality and how
the aspirant must rise beyond ordinary experience and ordinary responses to be one with it: even – for Hindu tradition
does not shrink from this – beyond the guidance of the sacred
texts themselves. It is a testimony to the value Hindu mysticism placed on independence that the Upanishads and

other texts exhort aspirants to transcend scripture itself in the search for one's own destiny.

The second text, Atma Upanishad, offers a very simple and effective tripartite model of this transcendence. The human being exists in an outer world and an inner one, that is, in the physical body and environment and in the realms of mind; yet there is something beyond both. In describing the world within, the Atma does what all Upanishads do best: describe consciousness with subtlety, profundity, and humor. The realm beyond cannot be described at all, but the effects of knowing it are extolled.

The next text in this selection, Amritabindu, is one of four or five Upanishads whose names end in *bindu* or "drop," indicating their succinct distillation of wisdom. Amrita, "immortality," like its Greek cousin Ambrosia, was thought of in ritualistic and mythic contexts as a kind of liquid. This is not the Upanishad's conception. It concentrates on the mind as the seat of spiritual struggle. The mind is a "wondrous power," as Sri Ramana Maharshi said, and our destiny in life is determined by what we do with that power. The opening line of the Dhammapada, a central text of Theravada Buddhism, is "All that we are is the result of what we have thought" (more literally, of mind). If we neglect mind, the senses and lower forces in our inherited consciousness take control of it; if we train it carefully, we can utilize its power to liberation – to immortality.

The Paramahamsa Upanishad, last in our selection, stresses that the insignia of the religious pilgrim or mendicant are symbolic. Like the rituals observed by householders, they are at best aids to the conditions of freedom, love, and wisdom the seeker must establish within. In this regard the Paramahamsa resembles descriptions of true spirituality found, for example, in the last chapter of the Dhammapada ("The Brahmin") and still later in the poems of Kabir.

— M . N .

Lead me from the unreal to the Real.
Lead me from darkness to light.
Lead me from death to immortality.

OM *shanti shanti shanti*

II: *Four Minor Upanishads*

[1] Let us meditate on the shining Self,
Changeless, underlying the world of change,
And realized in the heart in samadhi.

[2] Hard to reach is the supreme goal of life,
Hard to describe and hard to abide in.
[3] They alone attain samadhi who have
Mastered their senses and are free from anger,
Free from self-will and from likes and dislikes,
Without selfish bonds to people and things.

[4] They alone attain samadhi who are
Prepared to face challenge after challenge
In the three stages of meditation.
Under an illumined teacher's guidance
They become united with the Lord of Love,
[5-6] Called Vishnu, who is present everywhere.

Though the three gunas emanate from him,
He is infinite and invisible.
Though all the galaxies emerge from him,
He is without form and unconditioned.

To be united with the Lord of Love
Is to be freed from all conditioning.
This is the state of Self-realization,
Far beyond the reach of words and thoughts.

To be united with the Lord of Love,
Imperishable, changeless, beyond cause
And effect, is to find infinite joy.
Brahman is beyond all duality,
Beyond the reach of thinker and of thought.

Let us meditate on the shining Self,
The ultimate reality, who is
Realized by the sages in samadhi.

Brahman cannot be realized by those
Who are subject to greed, fear, and anger.
Brahman cannot be realized by those
Who are subject to the pride of name and fame
Or to the vanity of scholarship.
Brahman cannot be realized by those
Who are enmeshed in life's duality.

But to all those who pierce this duality,
Whose hearts are given to the Lord of Love,
He gives himself through his infinite grace;
He gives himself through his infinite grace.

O M *shanti shanti shanti*

ATMA UPANISHAD

[1] This is the teaching of sage Angiras:

Purusha manifests itself three ways:
As outer, inner, and the supreme Self.
Skin, flesh, vertebral column, hair, fingers,
Toes, nails, ankles, stomach, navel, hips, thighs,
Cheeks, eyebrows, forehead, head, eyes, ears,
       arms, sides,
Blood vessels, nerves: these make up the outer self,
The body, subject to birth and death.

[2] The inner self perceives the outside world,
Made up of earth, water, fire, air, and space.
It is the victim of likes and dislikes,
Pleasure and pain, and delusion and doubt.
It knows all the subtleties of language,
Enjoys dance, music, and all the fine arts;
Delights in the senses, recalls the past,
Reads the scriptures, and is able to act.
This is the mind, the inner person.

[3] The supreme Self, adored in the scriptures,
Can be realized through the path of yoga.
Subtler than the banyan seed, subtler
Than the tiniest grain, even subtler

Than the hundred-thousandth part of a hair,
This Self cannot be grasped, cannot be seen.

The supreme Self is neither born nor dies.
He cannot be burned, moved, pierced, cut, nor dried.
Beyond all attributes, the supreme Self
Is the eternal witness, ever pure,
Indivisible, and uncompounded,
Far beyond the senses and the ego.
In him conflicts and expectations cease.
He is omnipresent, beyond all thought,
Without action in the external world,
Without action in the internal world.
Detached from the outer and the inner,
This supreme Self purifies the impure.

O M *shanti shanti shanti*

AMRITABINDU UPANISHAD

1 The mind may be said to be of two kinds,
Pure and impure. Driven by the senses
It becomes impure; but with the senses
Under control, the mind becomes pure.

2 It is the mind that frees us or enslaves.
Driven by the senses we become bound;
Master of the senses we become free.
3 Those who seek freedom must master their senses.

4 When the mind is detached from the senses
One reaches the summit of consciousness.
5 Mastery of the mind leads to wisdom.
Practice meditation. Stop all vain talk.
6 The highest state is beyond reach of thought,
For it lies beyond all duality.

7 Keep repeating the ancient mantram O M
Until it reverberates in your heart.

8 Brahman is indivisible and pure;
Realize Brahman and go beyond all change.
9 He is immanent and transcendent.
Realizing him, sages attain freedom
10 And declare there are no separate minds.
They have but realized what they always are.

[11] Waking, sleeping, dreaming, the Self is one.
Transcend these three and go beyond rebirth.

[12] There is only one Self in all creatures.
The One appears many, just as the moon
Appears many, reflected in water.

[13] The Self appears to change its location
But does not, just as the air in a jar
Changes not when the jar is moved about.
[14] When the jar is broken, the air knows not;
But the Self knows well when the body is shed.

[15] We see not the Self, concealed by maya;
When the veil falls, we see we are the Self.

[16] The mantram is the symbol of Brahman;
Repeating it can bring peace to the mind.

[17] Knowledge is twofold, lower and higher.
Realize the Self; for all else is lower.
[18] Realization is rice; all else is chaff.

[19] The milk of cows of any hue is white.
The sages say that wisdom is the milk
And the sacred scriptures are the cows.

[20] As butter lies hidden within milk,
The Self is hidden in the hearts of all.

Churn the mind through meditation on it;
[21] Light your fire through meditation on it:
The Self, all whole, all peace, all certitude.

[22] "I have realized the Self," declares the sage,
"Who is present in all beings.
I am united with the Lord of Love;
I am united with the Lord of Love."

OM *shanti shanti shanti*

PARAMAHAMSA UPANISHAD

[1] Narada enquired of the Lord of Love:
"What is the state of the illumined one?"
The Lord replied: "Hard to reach is the state
Of the illumined one. Only a few
Attain it. But even one is enough.
For he is the pure Self of the scriptures;
He is truly great because he serves me,
And I reveal myself through him always."

He has renounced all selfish attachments
And observes no rites and ceremonies.
He has only minimum possessions,
And lives his life for the welfare of all.

[2] He has no staff nor tuft nor sacred thread.
He faces heat and cold, pleasure and pain,
Honor and dishonor with equal calm.
He is not affected by calumny,
Pride, jealousy, status, joy, or sorrow,
Greed, anger, or infatuation,
Excitement, egoism, or other goads;
For he knows he is neither body nor mind.

Free from the sway of doubt and false knowledge
He lives united with the Lord of Love,

Who is ever serene, immutable,
Indivisible, the source of all joy
And wisdom. The Lord is his true home,
His pilgrim's tuft of hair, his sacred thread;
For he has entered the unitive state.

³ Having renounced every selfish desire,
He has found his rest in the Lord of Love.
Wisdom is the staff that supports him now.
Those who take a mendicant's staff while they
Are still at the mercy of their senses
Cannot escape enormous suffering.
The illumined man knows this truth of life.

⁴ For him the universe is his garment
And the Lord not separate from himself.
He offers no ancestral oblations;
He praises nobody, blames nobody,
Is never dependent on anyone.

He has no need to repeat the mantram,
No more need to practice meditation.
The world of change and changeless Reality
Are one to him, for he sees all in God.

The aspirant who is seeking the Lord
Must free himself from selfish attachments
To people, money, and possessions.

When his mind sheds every selfish desire,
He becomes free from the duality
Of pleasure and pain and rules his senses.
No more is he capable of ill will;
No more is he subject to elation,
For his senses come to rest in the Self.
Entering into the unitive state,
He attains the goal of evolution.
Truly he attains the goal of evolution.

O M *shanti shanti shanti*

❐ *A Religion for Modern Times*

BY MICHAEL N. NAGLER

THE UPANISHADS HAVE OFTEN BEEN called the purest source of India's spiritual tradition. If we take the word *pure* to mean that they consist of essentials and are not tangled up in the changing circumstances of the culture that produced and recorded them, we will see why they are not only still revered in India but have been discovered by individuals throughout the world as treasures of needed wisdom – even though they are not particularly easy to read.

Our age seems to need this kind of guidance more than ever. We are passing through a spiritual crisis that has been brought about by a wrong message about human nature and human happiness – a message so pervasive that it makes up a global culture of its own. We need to turn to sources of wisdom wherever we can find them. Against this backdrop the wisdom tradition in general is indispensable, and the Upanishads in particular have some attractive features recommending them as a way to mine that tradition and integrate the best it has to offer into our modern lives.

First, the Upanishads offer a noble, exalted vision of human

Michael Nagler is Professor Emeritus of Classics & Comparative Literature, University of California, Berkeley.

nature. To hear sages say, "Hear, O children of immortal bliss, you are born to be united with the Lord," or to read the many "ladder" images in the texts that show us that our awareness of ourselves as physical bodies is a mere shadow of what we really are, brings a shock of recognition, a great relief.

Second, while the Upanishads are wrapped in a good bit of mythology and ritual, that wrapping comes off pretty easily. What we are left with is pure mysticism: a penetrating and remarkably comprehensive vision of Truth that can give us inspiration and a direction – a beckoning goal and a way to reach it.

Third, the Upanishads are scientific and experiential. They don't say, "believe this"; they say, "This we have seen: if you do x, y, and z, you can confirm it for yourself." They offend neither our sense of logic nor our sense of responsibility for discovering truth for ourselves. More: their outlook is nonjudgmental. They speak with fervor about darkness and ignorance, not with indignation about sin. They give us their glorious testimony about reality and let us decide whether we want to realize it for ourselves. Their universe is rigorously unforgiving in the sense that ignorance is its own punishment, and rigorously redemptive in the sense that wisdom is its own reward.

All this being said about the Upanishad's universality, the fact remains that these conversations (as they seem to have been) were recorded very far back in time in a world that was very different from our own. They do require some getting used to. My familiarity with them grew as I learned more about the world from which they had come; and this is what I will now try to share.

I. SONGS OF TRUTH:

WHAT IS AN UPANISHAD?

An Upanishad is an utterance of mystical truth that has come down to us as an attachment to the Vedas, the ancient and extremely sacred hymn collections or Samhitas of the Indo-Aryans. These collections are four in number – Rig, Yajur, Sama, and Atharva, in order of their age and their predominant interest in gods, ritual formula, chant, or magic spells. They and their adjuncts of almost equally ancient material form the textual basis to this day of India's major religious system. To be Hindu means in some sense to accept their authority, and since Hinduism is a decentralized system with diffuse institutional controls, there is almost no other criterion. As one studies the Upanishads today it is useful to keep in view this seeming paradox of decentralized authority and unwritten stability .

Veda (etymologically "sacred knowledge," or wisdom) means in the first instance these four Samhitas or collections of inspired hymns directed to the gods of the Indo-Aryan pantheon and divinized aspects of the Vedic religious ideology, such as fire, as well as some hymns so elusive we can no longer tell what exactly they are celebrating. A second meaning of the word includes three classes of texts which were soon attached to, and preserved with, their respective Samhitas. The first are the Brahmanas, lengthy descriptions of the Vedic rituals in a prose which is nearly that of classical Sanskrit, containing a vast amount of lore and narrative from innumerable family traditions. These texts were basically manuals for the priests (also *brahmanas,* "brahmins") responsible for the increasingly complex family and community rites. Second is a smaller and more intriguing group of texts known as Aranyakas or "forest manuals," continuations of the Brahmanas but "dealing with the speculations and spirituality of forest dwellers . . . , those who have renounced the world."[1] And third are the earliest Upanishads or "confidential sessions."[2] The Upanishads thus consummate a line of development which begins with the official hymns of the extended family that were recited at their public rituals and ends with utterances of universal import that a remarkable class of forest sages had given to their intimate disciples. For this reason, and because they are handed down at the end of the Vedic collections and are meant to be learned and recited last by Vedic students, the Upanishads are classified as *vedānta,* "the end of the Vedas."

Indian tradition makes a distinction between the Samhitas and Brahmanas, which deal mainly with ritual performance, and the Aranyakas and Upanishads, especially the latter, which deal with interpretation: what the rituals, and then what things in general, mean. The technical terms for these two divisions were *karma kanda* and *jnana kanda,* the portions dealing respectively with (ritual) action and spiritual knowledge. In the Upanishads themselves the former often serves as foil for the latter; that is, rituals become symbols of Self-realization, always an elusive state to describe in words.

However they began, there are today about two hundred texts which go by the name of Upanishad – or, according to another classification, one hundred and eight, an auspicious number in Hinduism. Looked at as a genre, these texts vary as drastically in content and spirituality as they do in age, ranging from the oldest prose Upanishads to some which are obviously medieval. The transcendent authority of the older texts rises above sectarian forms of religion to represent the religion that Hindus originally called not "Hinduism" but the *sanātana dharma* or "eternal law."

Early in the eighth century A.D., in a period when Hinduism was losing its bearings, the great mystic and philosopher Shankara, knowing that only mystical experience could reinvigorate the tradition, composed remarkable commentaries on ten of the Upanishads, giving them as it were a secondary canonization by his authority, labor, and vast intellectual achievement – and renewing Hinduism in the process. These ten Upanishads are listed by Indian tradition in the following order: Isha, Kena, Katha, Prashna, Mundaka, Mandukya, Taittiriya, Aitareya, Chandogya, Brihadaranyaka. The Shvetashvatara is no less treasured today, and some scholars say that Shankara wrote a commentary on it which has not survived. These eleven are commonly considered the principal Upanishads.

The class of people who taught in the forest ashrams of ancient India were "apparently engaged," as D. S. Sarma points out, "in the mighty task of transforming a rather low type of sacrificial religion prevalent at the time into a great mystical religion true for all time."[3] It would be misleading to say there was no trace of mysticism in the Samhitas; wherever there is a real love of life there is a groundwork of mystical devotion, and the exuberance of the hymns, their total faith in the order of the universe (*rita*) and in man's place in nature, seen and unseen, their sense of the seriousness of human action – all these belong to a spirit of mysticism. Besides, the Samhitas and especially the oldest, the Rig Veda Samhita, contain impressive profundity in speculation about the nature of being, time, and the universe, as in the famous *Nāsādīya Sūkta* (.129.1.4), sometimes called a "basis of the Upanishads":[4]

> At first there was neither Being nor Nonbeing.
> There was not air nor yet sky beyond.
> What was its wrapping? Where? In whose protection?
> Was water there, unfathomable and deep?
> In the beginning Love arose,
> Which was the primal germ cell of the mind.
> The seers, searching in their hearts with wisdom,
> Discovered the connection of Being in Nonbeing.
> Who really knows? Who can presume to tell it?
> Whence was it born? Whence issued this creation?
> Even the gods came after its emergence.
> Then who can tell from whence it came to be?

The Vedas give us glimpses into a mythological world which looks like that of Greece, Rome, and the rest of Europe, but different. The Upanishadic universe also contains "three worlds," but these are not the underworld, "middle-earth," and heaven as in the West, but the visible world, heaven (or the sky), and another plane that is far beyond phenomenal reality. The human being is not a puny speck in this cosmos, as we may appear physically. By virtue of a power called *tapas* ("heat") generated by extreme austerity (also called *tapas*) or in deep stages of meditation, ordinary men or women can compel profound changes in the universe. The hard line between mortality and immortality, between mankind and the gods, which Greek and Roman religion hammer home, is blurred and crossable.

When we get to the Upanishads themselves there is a new element, something almost disconcertingly different. It can be brought out in an image which appears in the Rig Veda (I.164.20) and is repeated, sometimes verbatim, in several Upanishads:

> Two birds of beautiful plumage, comrades
> Inseparable, live on the selfsame tree.
> One bird eats the fruit of pleasure and pain;
> The other looks on without eating.

When this image occurs in the Vedic context it's pretty clear that the bird that does partake – that is, the person who enjoys the fruits of life – is being held up for praise. In the Upanishadic contexts it is just the other way around: he or she who is not hypnotized by the ever-changing stream of phenomena but observes it in detachment is heading for the supreme human destiny.

Sometimes the Upanishads draw attention to this discontinuity with a boldness of thought few cultures – not to say religions – have ventured, as when they openly state that the Vedas themselves are only aids to realization which an already realized person no longer needs (Mundaka I.2.7). One way of looking at the decisive difference is that the religion of the Samhitas centers on the gods, and the direct, enthusiastic invocation and worship of them at the sacrifice.

In the Brahmanas, however, the intense power of the sacrifice itself (the original meaning of *brahman*) becomes the focus, and the sacrifice which moves the gods is several times said to be more powerful than they are. Then, finally, in the Aranyakas, power is seen to rest in man himself. There is a ground for mysticism in the Samhitas, but only the Aranyakas and then decisively the Upanishads plant in that ground and cultivate it systematically.

It is because of this fundamental commitment to spiritual values and the focus on human consciousness that the Upanishads may be regarded as the source, insofar as texts are the source, of India's civilization. There is a mystical element at the heart of all great religious systems; but in India that mysticism has been established and systematically developed, to become – to use a phrase of Schopenhauer's – "the faith of the people."

However this happened, mysticism and the intense devotion that is always a part of mysticism have become the heart of India's civilization, and if it survives the current corrosion of values by materialism the way it survived, in centuries past, the successive attacks of Mongols, Muslims, and British, the spiritual culture of India will be a precious resource for a world reawakening to the need for spiritual values. But for this to happen, some difficulties that lie in the path of our understanding this culture must be cleared. Perhaps the most serious is simply the rarity of the experience they are attempting to describe. To this day, only a rare few human beings have actually had the experience of "seeing" reality from the perspective taken by these remarkable documents. The Self is "hidden in the deepest cave of the heart." It cannot be perceived by the senses, like phenomena we can measure or describe. We have to build a road into the regions of consciousness where we can "see" what lies there; we need an appropriate and sufficiently powerful organ of perception, what the Bhagavad Gita (11.8) calls the "divine eye." It is for this reason that the author of the Kena exclaims, "We do not know, we do not understand." (1.3).

II. INDIAN CULTURE & TRADITION

Rabindranath Tagore once pointed out that while the Greeks and Romans built great cities, India's was a "forest civilization."[5] Not that there were no great cities in ancient India – Harappa and Mohenjo Daro rose and fell before Mycenaean palaces were erected on the Greek mainland – but the essential continuity of the culture was developed and preserved by families living in small communities close to nature long after splendid palaces and universities rose in those cities. This had profound consequences, as Tagore explains, for the Hindu worldview. Like the Hebrews, the ancient Indians distrusted the pace and pomp of urbandom, and distrusted it enough to resist central authority and conformism for thousands of years. Their trust in oral creativity and preservation paid off, for India's is an extremely well-documented civilization. More survives of classical Sanskrit than of ancient Greek and perhaps Latin literature put together: the Iliad, the Odyssey, and the Aeneid would fit into one vast Indian epic, the Mahabharata, with room to spare for Lucian and some others.

These choices help to explain what meets us in the Upanishads: their intimacy, the bewildering variety of their outer form, the fact that they are creative utterances of gifted individuals, even the way they were preserved as a precious inheritance in family traditions. It is this closeness to the individual person that makes them, behind an austere facade, deeply devotional.

The Upanishads are in some ways the archetype for other forms of Indian culture, most importantly perhaps in their grounding in the teacher-student relationship. Not only in mysticism, but in Indian music and other arts it is this reliance on person-to-person communication, both for teaching the individual student and for perpetuating the *parampara* or "succession" that keeps the art alive for the whole culture.

Indian aesthetics holds that the essence of every moment in an artistic performance is its *rasa,* which corresponds to one of nine moods or dispositions, such as fear, erotic love, or devotion. If the Upanishads are an archetypal art form in that sense, what is their rasa? That question occupied Indian aestheticians a great deal, and their answer was skillful: the Upanishads come from the disposition of *shānta,* "peace," which is not really a disposition or mood but what happens when all mental dispositions are brought to rest: again the Upanishads are an "end of the Vedas."

The rasa theory also allowed Indian theorists to get a grip on what an Upanishad was essentially, rather than formally: whenever you have a truth-utterance (a profound statement by someone in a higher state of consciousness) you have an Upanishad. In this sense the Bhagavad Gita is an Upanishad, and the epic in which it is embedded, the Mahabharata, however violent on the surface, itself teaches detachment from worldly gain and communicates the predisposition of inner calm (*shama*) leading also to spiritual peace (*shanta*).[6]

This attention to theory and classification bring us to the fact that India's was a highly scientific spirit, and this combination of science and devotion, of detached observation and mystical ecstasy, is one of the most arresting – and useful – aspects of the Upanishads. It did not stop with them. When Gandhi told the world that he had been instructed to undertake his "epic fast" in 1932 by "the voice of God," many asked how he knew he was not having a hallucination. He calmly told them, "The claim that I have made is neither extraordinary nor exclusive. God will rule the lives of all those who surrender themselves without reservation to him." And he added, "Here is no question of hallucination. I have stated a simple, scientific law that can be verified by anyone who will carry out the necessary preparations. . . ." We are used to considering religion and science at odds – a divorce that many consider very harmful. Gandhi's confident claim is an arresting revelation, entirely in the spirit of the Upanishads.

If we judge a theory by its explanatory power, one of the most successful in the Upanishads is the theory of prana. The word may

come from the prefix *pra-* "forth" (possibly used here as an inten-
sifier) and the important root *an* "to breathe." As generally used,
prana means "(living) energy": all the "vital signs" by which we try
to identify the presence of life are tokens of the capacity of a body
to direct, conserve, and employ energy at a high level of complexity. The Upanishadic sages worked out the primacy of prana over its
various functions in the body by what we call thought-experiments.
One might imagine, for example, what would happen if the individual faculties (in Sanskrit, *indriyas*) leave a person one by one: as
sight leaves, the person would go blind, and so forth, but still live.
This is exactly what we find in the Brihadaranyaka (VI.1.7–13) and
other Upanishads. But when prana itself makes ready to leave, "like
a great stallion pulling up the stakes by which he was tethered," all
the faculties gather round and beg it to remain, declaring they have
learned their lesson: they all derive their existence from prana. Or
one might imagine what would happen if all the faculties left and
came *back* to the inert body one by one: how would sight function
by itself if one were not conscious? This is the Aitareya experiment,
and there are others in the Prashna and elsewhere. The sages are
saying, as it were, "If our theory is correct, death should only occur
when prana itself goes, and conversely life should resume when it
returns."

The sages testify that they have confirmed all this by direct observation – but that observation requires a highly trained observer.
This is a principle known in Western medieval philosophy as *adae-
quatio rei et intellectu,* the "suitability of the cognitive equipment

to its task": the senses and the mind (which Indians considered the chief sense) must be brought to a stillness, usually by assiduous training, in order for us to become aware of prana and what lies beyond even that.

In giving us these thought-experiments the sages probably had three things in mind. First and foremost, they wanted to guide the cognitive growth of others who could be inspired to undertake the training required to perceive the life-process in this direct way. Second, they simply wanted to explain life with the most powerful theory, which is why they are so rigorously logical. And finally they meant to put a science of health on a firm basis – in other words, to say something true and useful about the process and the systems we call life. From this scientific basis the sages were also able to explain, again drawing on their incredible skill at directing attention inward, the fivefold distribution of the body's energy, which is elaborated, including its relationship to other realities, in the Prashna and several other Upanishads.

I hope I have illustrated that with a little getting used to, one can move around handily enough in the Indian system, which was quite scientific and rational in its own terms. Diversity is not disharmony. Without formal rules, Hindus organized a vast collection of texts into categories and canonized them in a system that was authoritative throughout Hindu culture. In this respect India invites comparison with another ancient people with intense spiritual longings who remained decentralized, not by choice but by the destruction of their political integrity: the Jews. In this description of the Mishnaic inheritance we might almost be reading a description of the Upanishads:[7]

> The Talmud is the repository of thousands of years of Jewish wisdom, and the oral law, which is as ancient and significant as the written law (the Torah), finds expression therein. It is a conglomerate of law, legend, and philosophy, a blend of unique logic and shrewd pragmatism, of history and science, anecdotes and humor. It is a collection of paradoxes: its framework is orderly and logical, every word and term subjected to meticulous editing, completed centuries after the actual work of composition came to an end; yet it is still based on free association, on a harnessing together of diverse ideas reminiscent of the modern stream-of-consciousness novel.

Even more than diaspora Jewish tradition, the survival strategy of Indian culture was cumulative. This is a particularly useful generalization to bear in mind. India was probably the only country where three in many ways contradictory systems of medicine, Indian, Arabic, and Greek, flourished side by side; a similar toleration extended to the successive stages of evolution in religious consciousness through which India passed. Outworn forms of religious worship were virtually never discarded – as Professor Sarma points out, the sages did their job of moving people beyond their "rather low type of sacrificial religion . . . without in any explicit manner breaking away from the traditions of the past."[8]

The resulting accumulation can be confusing because most traditions have not been cumulative; they reject a "creed outworn" when they move on to a new stage. The ability to accommodate rather than reject older beliefs has a very practical outcome. India has had its share of religious intolerance, but thanks to its paradigm of unity-in-diversity and its cumulative strategy for preserving culture, those individuals and communities who respond to outward forms of worship have kept their place and dignity in the system, while at the other extreme individuals who have really had mystical experience have been unusually free to transcend all religious forms and not only follow their own path but become beacons for the culture as a whole. "As men approach me, so I receive them," Sri Krishna says in the Gita. "All paths, Arjuna, lead to me" (Gita 4.11). This too helps explain the mixtures, or more properly layers, of religious consciousness displayed in the Upanishads.

III. THE LITERARY VEHICLE

Although not many of the Upanishadic passages dealing with ritual and sacrifice are included in this or most other modern collections, the texts' concern with that aspect of religion went beyond the fact that technically the Upanishads are commentaries on the Vedas. Ritual stood for all human action; sacrifice, once internalized, was the key idea of mysticism and thus became a perfect vehicle of continuity between the Brahmanas and the texts' own interiorizing mystical vision. In the Upanishads' treatment of sacrifice we can learn many things about how they work as literary, philosophical, and religious texts.

Many Upanishadic passages have to be interpreted by two or

more "codes" (as literary critics say today), since a new set of mean-ings is mapped onto an older set of symbols.[9] The gods or devas of the natural world are dramatizations of phenomena like rain and wind, but they also stand for parallel faculties in the human being. When Krishna says in the Gita, "Those who worship the gods go to the gods, but my devotees come to me" (Gita 7. 23), he means that those who live in the sense-world end up stuck in the sense-world; but those who try to reach awareness of their inner Self become completely realized.

At all stages of Indian civilization the world-process itself was considered a sacrifice. Even the gods carry out sacrifice, playing, just as human beings must, their role in the continuation of the cosmic cycle. But as we have seen, *devas* can stand for the sensory and motor faculties, divine energy as experienced in the micro-cosm; Shankara elsewhere comments, "It is a fact established on the strength of the scriptures that speech and the other faculties are conscious through being presided over by conscious deities."[10] So in this image of the gods offering sacrifice for the continuity of the cosmic process (or *as* that process) we also can see the beginnings of one of the most important principles of mysticism, the principle of yajna or spiritual sacrifice: in order to reach the highest fulfillment, the human being returns vital energy to the process rather than clinging to it. In practical terms, he or she works for the well-being of the world rather than for the gratification of personal desires, and therefore even eating is ideally a sacrifice meant to empower a self-less contribution to the world process. We encounter this repeatedly in the Upanishads; the Fourth Question of the Prashna contains just this allegory of human life as sacrifice, and the spiritual principle of yajna is, as Gandhi said, the essence of the Isha, indeed of India's civilization.

Likewise, when the Upanishads describe the soul as traveling through various realms after death, they are really referring to realms of psychic experience we can have in this life. The Upanishads do not suppress but reuse the complex layers of symbolic thought they have inherited. If their interest in sacrifices was a debt owed to their Vedic and Brahmanic home in the literary tradition, it was a debt they paid cheerfully, for it gave them a perfect vehicle for their new message.

In the Katha and some other Upanishads we come across an expression that means literally "eating up the good works" (*karma*) of someone or other. *Karma* means primarily the spiritual or ethically operational residue of every act. Thus not only a ritual act but every act is symbolic, in the sense that beyond its external, visible effects are the far more important, deep-residing effects of every thought, word, and deed on our spiritual relationships.

These effects entangle us in further relationships, making up our network – or net – of karma. Yet, as the Gita so eloquently says (3.4–6), it is absurd to think we have a choice not to act; even if we sit quietly our thoughts and desires will go on driving through the world of karmic influence. How can we ever be free of such a tangle? Precisely by learning more and more day by day to act in a spirit of yajna.

It was Gandhi who really brought this abstruse doctrine back to vibrant life: act, by all means, but make your act, in the modern sense of the word, a sacrifice. That is, he explained, choose a selfless goal, use right means (nonviolence), and never be pushed into action for your own benefit – a tall order. Gandhi was not waxing metaphorical when he called his programs for the deliverance of India – and of the individual activist – yajna. By drawing upon the not-to-be-denied need in all of us to work for a selfless goal he elevated even his political campaigns to the level of models for every action we might want to take today.

What Professor Sarma called the sages' "mighty task" of making the Hindu system valid for all time could be expressed in a single word: *interiorization*. Interiorization does not mean giving up on external struggles and satisfactions but rather reaching the center of the field where all satisfaction is ultimately achieved for us human beings. It does not mean losing life; it means the sacrificer gets eternal life. The Upanishads share with all sages the same high vision of what the human being can become: without sacrifice, we stop short of something that is essentially human.

Several things about the Vedic sacrificial (and, more generally, ritual) belief system made it relatively easy to develop that system mystically – that is, to interiorize it. At an early stage, for example, a certain type of priest was designated who officiated at the rituals mentally, not participating in the acts or recitations but going through them in his mind.[11] His role originally was the important one of protecting the performance against errors, which were felt to be dangerous and required elaborate purification; but that precedent of an interior run-through led to the provision that one could actually perform the rituals mentally if the necessary implements or personnel were not available – for example, in the forest. It was a relatively short step from this provision to the position that as far as the true purpose of religion goes, external rites – however suitable for the short-term resolution of social problems – are unnecessary, or at best symbolic. The real sacrifice could then be done directly, not just attempted by symbolic manipulations.

At the beginning of the Katha Upanishad we seem to have a recapitulation of this historic process. Everything it describes has more than one meaning. Nachiketa, a forthright youth who takes life seriously, is taken aback by his father's sham sacrifice, but underneath he is actually frustrated with the unreality of the world. His longing and his sincerity bring him face to face with the power of death. Given three boons, he chooses first of all to be reconciled with his father and to escape the immediate danger of death he is facing. Then – his relationship to death is becoming that of spiritual aspirant before the supreme teacher – he asks and receives the knowledge of the fire sacrifice that "leads to heaven." Then with the third boon comes the point: "O Death, having seen your face, how can I enjoy anything again? Teach me the real secret: What are you? What happens when we die, and how can we not?" He does not want to die and come back to life; he does not want to die and be remembered; finally he just does not want to die.

And he does not have to. Desire focused and unified at that depth opens for him "the entire secret of meditation" (Katha II.3.18) by which one leaves all separate individuality – and consequently all that is created and must die – behind. These stages of the story reflect rather well the development of India's rich, complex, and cumulative religious history, driven always by the quenchless desire for life that caused it to evolve into one of the most highly developed – and inspiring – systems of mysticism in the world.

We think of the Upanishads first and foremost as a well of deep meaning – their practical use to and effect upon us. But Indian pundits and scholars of old considered them also as a source of poetic beauty, and this beauty is not entirely secondary. The Upanishads inherit from the Vedas a capacity for inspired poetry. They speak, usually, in a less lyrical voice; on the other hand, they have even deeper access to the basic resource of all poetry, which is vision. Vision often produces poetry even when the Upanishads speak in their most dogged prose; for example in highly imaginative imagery that can suddenly light up an elusive concept with deceptive simplicity (see the introduction, p. 15). These images stay in the mind; once we hear them, we will carry them around like a torch, throwing light on life wherever we live it. When we understand the purpose of the Upanishads and have grown used to their aesthetic, reading them can be what it was meant to be: a deeply enjoyable, moving, and even transformative experience.

IV. THE PHILOSOPHY

To modern ears the word *philosophy* connotes a kind of dry, theoretical learning which would be almost a travesty of the Upanishads' passion for experiential realization. As the sages used the term, knowing is not a separate activity from other aspects of being – courage, endurance, concentration, will. There is such a thing as mere intellectual knowing, of course, but the Mundaka Upanishad, for example, begins by setting aside this kind of knowing as *apara*, "nontranscendent" – that is, not dealing with transformative experience. The Upanishads are concerned with *para*, "transcendent" knowledge, "by knowing which, all things are known" (I.3) in a way that our being and our actions are transformed. For this kind of knowledge there were four nonintellectual prerequisites: discrimination, detachment, self-control, and an "irrepressible hankering after the realization of truth."[12]

Ordinary knowledge is either subjective or objective; transcendent knowing is neither. When a student in the Upanishads says, for example, "I did not know that such-and-such is Brahman," he means he has not yet *realized* the identity of that thing with its source, precisely because he has been seeing it as a separate object. But according to mysticism – and to modern physics – we cannot know anything objectively; it does not really exist independently of an observer, where both observer and observed are participating in consciousness.

On the other hand, neither can we know things subjectively as yet, because that would only be superimposing our own preconceived ideas on things. The only way we can truly know something is to become identified with it. We can become what we would know. "If [one] loves a stone, he becomes a stone; if he loves a man, he is a man; if he loves God – I dare not say more, for if I said that he would then be God, you might stone me."[13] This, minus the final hesitation, is precisely the position of the sages.

The higher mode of knowing induced by intense selfless love and identification produces powerful changes in the knower: "Whatever they [knowers of Brahman] desire, the object of that desire arises from the power of their own thoughts; they have it and are happy" (Chandogya VIII.2.1–10). If these claims overdraw on the credulity of the modern reader, it is because we think naturally of the normal mode of knowing with which we are familiar. Earlier translators used to think the Upanishads were talking about magic, especially when the symbolic code of the text happens to concern ritual: "He who performs this rite *knowing* goes beyond death." What the sages mean is that if one sees through the symbolism of the ritual to its meaning *and* identifies with that inner core of meaning through spiritual union, rites become superfluous. For that knower they have fulfilled their purpose; they have lifted the performer's vision to the world beyond death. Spiritual identification is caught from rather than taught by an illumined teacher. "Knowing" in the Upanishads is a code for that realization.

Tradition has isolated four powerful formulaic utterances (*mahāvākyas*) embedded in the early Upanishads. One is *sarvam idam brahma,* "All is Brahman" (Chandogya III.14.1), which states the foundation of mysticism: that everything is ultimately one. In the Vedic period, that belief had taken the form of a great myth in which Purusha, or the prototypical "Person," was made into our world by the primordial sacrifice; his head became the Brahmin class, his arms the Kshatriyas or ruler-warriors, and so forth. We can say two things about the purport of this myth: it affirms the unity of life in a common source (Christian writers would make the same point about our common ancestor, Adam), and it affirms the *order,* or meaning, in the Universe: there is rita – harmony, regularity – underlying all seemingly random change. And that harmony or order prevails not only in the material order, making science possible; it is also seen in the laws that govern the conscious or moral dimensions of existence.[14]

What the myth does *not* tell us, being a myth, is the most important consequence of these beliefs: that a human being can reverse the process of creation which proceeded from singularity to diversity: not just retrace it, for example, in science or philosophy, but reverse it, so that one withdraws from the world of change and follows what St. Augustine called the "hidden footprint of unity" that is there, perhaps covered but never eradicated in our consciousness. [15]

The Upanishads never stray far from this purpose. Take the episode of Uddalaka and his son Shvetaketu (Chandogya VI.1–16). The latter has come home from his traditional twelve years' study under a brahmin teacher "proud of his learning in the scriptures" but unaware of the purpose of that learning. In this case the father must be his real teacher. Uddalaka first shakes him out of his complacency with a spiritual version of "What did you learn at school": "Did they teach you That by which everything else is known?" Then, as soon as the boy is ready to grasp that truth of truths, he has him dissolve salt in water, dissect a mustard seed, and perform other experiments that by analog or induction yield insights into the one Reality underlying all phenomena. These are not chemistry or biology lessons: each time Shvetaketu has such a flash of insight Uddalaka tells him, "Shvetaketu, you are That."

This is one of the central passages in the Upanishads, and its teaching that the supreme Reality can be found in the humblest and most ordinary objects "as fire lies hidden in firestick, butter in cream, water in springs" (Shvetashvatara I.15) is fundamental in the Upanishadic worldview. Not surprisingly, "You are That" (*tat tvam asi*) is one of the mahavakyas.[16]

Shvetaketu's sudden awakening is uncharacteristic; in most anagogic passages of the Upanishads the process is by gradual stages. When King Janaka asks Yajnavalkya, "What is the light of man?" (Brihadaranyaka IV.3.11 ff), the sage first cites the sources of visible light – sun, moon, fire – in diminishing order of brightness. Then he moves on to speech, by which we can "see" in the sense we can orient ourselves and carry out actions even in darkness. Finally he comes to the Self. That Self, Reality, or the divine ground of existence, does indeed exist in all things, or they would not exist; but to discover it we must slowly learn to peel back layers of reality like an onion.

There is an endless variety of such hierarchies in the Upanishads, all with a common pattern. They move from the inanimate world to some forms of consciousness (seeing, speech) to consciousness itself, or from outer things to our awareness of things – or feelings, or thoughts – to our Self, the ultimate witness. We are always being led back to that center from whatever perimeter to which the endless outward migrations of the mind have carried us.

This can be sometimes put, at least at first, in objective terms, because stacked up behind everything we perceive is the series of causes that brought it into existence, beginning with the First Cause of phenomenal existence itself (Katha 1.3.10). At the heart of any apparently separate thing lurks its essence – its rasa, literally "sap" – that brought that thing into being. When we see the essence, the thing itself has served its purpose: in the earthy language of the Upanishads, "the subtle eats the gross."[17] The rasa of anything is subtler than it; it is its cause, its explanation, and the key to its significance; it is more real – more long-lasting – and the next step closer to the ultimate reality beyond both the knower and the known.

But it is more illuminating to look at the theory in subjective terms. Behind the act lies the motive; the former in the world of material interaction, the latter in the world of thought and desire. In one sense the "cause" of the light in my study is electricity; in a more important sense it is my wish to have it there. If I fall asleep, there will be no "light" in the room: it's a participatory study, in this participatory universe.

All search for essences and for the ultimate relationship ends with *Atman,* the Self. This concept is the glory of the Upanishads. The etymology of the word is not entirely certain, but most likely it is derived from *an,* "to breathe," and thus shares an important linguistic as well as philosophical connection with prana. This richness of meaning is testimony to the very simplicity of the concept. Atman just means "self"; in Sanskrit it was used as the reflexive pronoun. Yet so much is contained within that simple concept: untold energy and devotion, the explanatory power of a scientific formula, the evocative power of poetry, and finally the sheer drama of the tremendous discovery made by the sages over and over again – one of the most authoritatively verified hypotheses in the universe – that the Self is God.

This Self cannot possibly be subject to any change, not even death. This is perhaps why belief in reincarnation died hard even in the West. It was a cherished belief not only in pagan but in various Jewish and Christian groups in the early centuries of our era, but was brusquely rejected by the emerging orthodoxy and seems an unsettling and unverifiable hypothesis to most of us today. Yet it differs only slightly, almost by a question of semantics, from the modern concept of evolution, which holds that the individual dies with the death of the physical body. Indian religious systems hold as a core belief that the individual is not that which dies: it is more accurate to think of ourselves as the forces which brought our body and personality into existence – forces that will continue shaping our destiny beyond what we call death, "as the wind takes on the fragrance from the flower" (Gita 15.8).

The ultimate Self, however, never entered into any of these processes but somehow governs them all. It is neither that which dies nor those shaping forces, but the Witness of all this evolution. The Self is untouched by the turmoil of the world, "observing without partaking" (the two birds' image), a bulwark that sorrow cannot broach (Chandogya VIII.4.1–2). Only because we think the Self is yoked to its temporary instruments, the body, mind, and senses, do we think it enjoys or dislikes anything in one little corner of the cosmic process (Katha 1.3.4). But it is present everywhere. The Self has "entered into everything like a razor fitted into its case" or (Augustine and St. Teresa use the same image) into every creature "up to the nails" (Brihadaranyaka 1.4.7). The Self alone has no essence, no cause, being the cause and essence of everything and everyone.

One might expect on the basis of such a revolutionary theory of being, or metaphysics, an equally well-developed theory of our relationship to things and people and how, if we have happiness in view, we ought to behave towards them. This expectation is not disappointed by the Upanishads, in which metaphysics and ethics are one.

The central value of Hinduism, declared in a formula known mostly from later narrative literature, is *ahimsā paramo dharma*: "The highest religion, the ultimate law of our being, is nonviolence." This value is implicit, and sometimes explicit (Chandogya IV.17.4) in the Upanishadic teaching of unity. Before we explore it, however, let us look at a complementary teaching which is equally surprising and perhaps even less easily understood.

One of the critical "secrets" of the Upanishads is that renunciation is the opposite of deprivation. When the senses (indriyas) are untrained they run wild, leading to a state of conditioning that is the opposite of freedom (Katha 1.2.5–6). Joy comes from putting these faculties back on track under the guidance of the Self. This is precisely why the Upanishads teach renunciation. Not only are joy and renunciation not contradictory; they positively require each other. Taken together they form the key value of Hinduism, as Mahatma Gandhi taught when he took for his own mahavakya those three opening words of the Isha Upanishad: *tena tyaktena bhuñjītāḥ*, "Renounce and enjoy."

In the Gita, desire is referred to once as the rasa of objects, i.e., the objects of sense experience (II.59, a verse which meant a very great deal to Gandhi). Since a thing's essence is more permanent than its material embodiment, it stands to reason that if we could somehow enjoy that essence directly, our enjoyment would be more permanent than sensory contact with the thing itself. A sense of joy and happiness within is longer-lasting than the sensation of pleasure, which is notoriously short-lived. One of the boldest treatments of this theory of satisfaction occurs in the Katha:

> That through which one enjoys form, sound, smell, taste, touch, and sexual union is the Self. Can there be anything not known to one who is the One in all? . . . That which enjoys the honey [rasa] from the flowers of the senses is the Self. (Katha II.1.3)

We lose nothing in this process; in St. Francis de Sales's fortuitous image, when the sun rises the light of a star does not go out, but "is ravished into and absorbed in the sun's sovereign light, within which it is happily mingled and allied."[18] Nor do the senses or the body generally suffer when we control them voluntarily. Free from the popular misconception about self-tormenting "yogis," Upanishadic students pray, "May my senses wax clear and strong." That is why they trained them.

This whole question is so important that I would like to make another pass through this logic, as the Upanishads would, from a slightly different point of view. If we could trace where a desire arises from – and the Upanishads do, repeatedly – we would find that in most cases something – a thought, an external event – has stirred up some wisp of the vague sense of incompleteness we harbor beneath the floor of surface consciousness as long as we are not identified with our Self. We immediately misinterpret this stirring as a desire for something outside us. This is maya: misinterpreting the longing for union within as a call from something outside the Self.

The Upanishads go a step further. When we have the sensation "I want such-and-such," what we really mean is that we want the relative tranquility that follows when that desire subsides. As a great sage of modern India, Sri Ramana Maharshi, who was very close to the Upanishads in spirit, once declared, "There is no happiness in any object of the world." The Self is pure happiness, which we mistake as coming from outside; so the closer we come to the Self within, the more we are aware of – the more we feel already – what we were looking for outside us. This is what the Upanishads mean by joy. "Renunciation" refers simply to dropping the outside reflection for the reality which is within.

Freedom is one of the most passionate concerns of the Upanishads, and a name of one of the oldest, Kaivalya.[19] But another Sanskrit word for freedom, *swaraj*, appears in the Chandogya as well as the Kaivalya, and this word was the rallying cry Mahatma Gandhi used in the successful Indian struggle for independence from British rule. Of course, what the Upanishads meant by *swaraj* was inner, personal freedom; but that is exactly what Gandhi meant by it too. "The word *swaraj* is a sacred word," he said, "a Vedic word, meaning self-rule and self-restraint, and not freedom from all restraint which 'independence' often means."

It is typical of the Upanishads' approach to life not to check or negate passions but to channel them, reconnecting them with their original source in deeper consciousness. In Upanishadic psychology, the inner demand all human beings feel for freedom is ultimately a drive to free ourselves from the inherited and acquired compulsions in our own psychic makeup. The Upanishads do not deny the need for political freedom; they simply claim that inner freedom comes first, and is really the only reliable guarantee of all other forms. The more freedom one wins within, through control over one's own thoughts and passions, the less one will be manipulable by others, and the more one will be able to seek political freedom – without going on to manipulate others oneself.

Thus we see that whereas the Upanishads were not *nitishastra*, textbooks of political counsel, they contained germs of profound richness for the alleviation of political and other relations. The imaginative setting of the Upanishads is a stable and perhaps idealized world of kings and brahmins (and birds and beasts, and gods), and the sages do not say much about how that world, much less one like ours, should be organized. Yet their feelings about those aspects of life also come through, sometimes in the most unexpected contexts. This passage is in the profoundly mystical eighth chapter of the Chandogya Upanishad:

> Here [in this world] people do what they are told, becoming
> dependent on their country, or their piece of land, or the
> desires of another, so their desires are not fulfilled and their
> works come to nothing, both in this world and in the next
> ... but those who leave here knowing who they are and
> what they truly desire have freedom everywhere, both in
> this world and in the next. (Chandogya VIII.1.5–6)

This modern-sounding scorn for "doing what you are told" comes as a bit of a shock in this stable world presided over by religious, family, and royal authority; but a closer look reveals that while the social structure of that world is stable, the sages don't hesitate to take this structure apart and show us where the underlying sources of authority are, or should be: more than one proud brahmin has to take lessons from a king who turns out to enjoy deeper spiritual experience (cp. Brihadaranyaka II.1.1–15); more than one teenager like Nachiketa pulls the wraps off a sham sacrifice or flings sham rewards back at the delighted king of death (cp. Katha). In this view freedom and authority come together, like renunciation and joy. The truly free man or woman is *svamin,* literally "in full possession of self." He or she exercises a spontaneous authority over others: not the authority that debases others but that ennobles them, not the authority that distances but that draws to intimacy, not the authority of birth or social advantage but of the ability to forget oneself in the welfare of others, which anyone can learn. "Real Swaraj will come," Gandhi said, "not by the acquisition of authority by a few, but by the acquisition of the capacity by all to resist authority when it is abused." Gandhi's last phrase shows how he had internalized the vision of the sages that in the ideal world, while there would have to be authority of each over himself, there could also be structures of authority among others, so long as these were exercised selflessly. The issue of authority is not, as often in our polarized world, yes or no, but what kind.

These basic principles lead naturally to two other "political" considerations, one of which we have touched on. Gandhi's "discovery" of nonviolence was Upanishadic to the core. It was an innate response to the at-homeness in the world that breathes through every line of those texts. And we find some principles of nonviolence well articulated: If one is socially or by personality weak with regard to another (that is, not yet svamin oneself), one still need not be exploited: "for by dharma even the weak man can hope to prevail against a king" (Brihadaranyaka 1.4.14, with Shankara's comment).[20] This dharma is nothing other than nonviolence; as we have seen, *ahimsā paramo dharma,* "There is no higher dharma than nonviolence." It is a fact not to be glossed over that Gandhi, one small man, prevailed against the British Empire in the height of its historic majesty with that secret. Can there be a secret more necessary to learn?

While various thinkers today have remarked how modern physics seems to reflect the vision of the forest sages, few have noticed how another significant discovery of ours was long anticipated by them: the concept of unity in diversity. Originally popularized by Hegel, this mildly paradoxical theme is becoming central in discussions of how a nation or even the world should be organized, for a very simple reason: the world needs, as Richard Falk has put it, "the maximum degree of spontaneous solidarity." But what kind of solidarity? A megagovernment? If this is to be world order, one may be excused for preferring chaos. When he begins to specify the requirements for true solidarity Professor Falk sounds almost Upanishadic: the goal must be "the maintenance of living systems at all levels of complexity . . . the exploration of space and the planetary character of economic, ecological, and cybernetic complexity are building the foundations of an inevitable global consciousness."[21] We want a new principle of political order which does not depend upon or induce uniformity among peoples, but which, tolerant of complexity, promotes the fullest unfolding of their individual potential – which happens to be a definition of nonviolence.[22]

The Upanishads of course specialize in diversity; in fact they revel in it as the essential character of life:

> He is this boy, he is that girl, he is this man, he is that
> woman, and he is this old man, too, tottering on his staff.
> His face is everywhere. He is the blue bird, he is the green
> bird with red eyes, he is the thundercloud, and he is the
> seasons and the sea. (Shvetashvatara IV.3–4)

But the forest vision of life balances this love of diversity in living beings with an unwavering focus on the unity which is life's center.

The concept of *dharma,* though not as developed in the Upanishads as in the narrative and sutra texts that followed, shows the same apparent tension between a universal Law unchanging in any time or circumstance – *the* dharma, properly speaking – and the less well known concept of *svadharma,* each individual's own law or way.[23] The Gita sternly describes how each must discover and earnestly follow his or her own path or perish spiritually: "competition in another's dharma breeds fear and insecurity" (Gita 3.35).

In the end, unity in diversity is not a paradox at all. Unity is the center – in Upanishadic terms, "in the cave of the heart" – of conscious beings, while diversity flourishes on the surface of life. It is as necessary to foster diversity there at the outside as it is to hold unity on the inside. Gandhi made this notion of inside and outside concrete for us: there must be "heart unity" among all, meaning spontaneous concern for the welfare of others, and that very concern must lead to complete toleration of natural differences and even differences of wealth and station (which did not please his Marxist critics) as long as they are not abused. Class, family, and regional groupings are a sort of bridge between the unity toward which all must be allowed to work and the individuality from which we start. The more the heart can be opened in spontaneous concern for the other, the less of an obstacle and more of a vehicle for social coherence – and in the end spiritual unity – intermediate unities become.[24]

Unity in diversity formed the cornerstone of India's national consciousness from ages past; it may yet form her contribution to a global consciousness which, as S. Radhakrishnan has said, the world has no choice but to develop.

V. THE CURVE OF HISTORY

Since the discovery of the Upanishads by the West, not a few Westerners have gone to them as a source of the "perennial philosophy," a fascinating witness to an ancient civilization and its unique religious system; others, like Yeats, have been drawn by their poetic beauty. But the first Western philosopher to stumble on them, Arthur Schopenhauer, was looking for much, much more. And they did not disappoint him. In his oft-quoted words: "They have been the consolation of my life, and will be the consolation of my death."[25]

It is not hard to appreciate his reaction. One of the closing statements in the first book of the Chandogya reads, "Whoever meditates and gains this wisdom here in this life lives at his highest and his best" (1.9.4), and Shankara comments, "People may think, 'Though such rewards might have accrued for the blessed ancients, they cannot be possible for people in this age.' The text proceeds to set aside this notion."

We too can set aside the notion that the Upanishads are irrelevant curiosities. Because of the intense problems of our times, problems that seem to be created by specifically modern conditions, we naturally tend to think we have broken the thread of history: Shankara did not have to face ecological degradation, terrorism, and nuclear war. But these problems arise from unresolved human difficulties that have been the same throughout recorded history. Ecological degradation is ultimately caused by human greed, as greed and alienation lie behind all forms of crime; war arises, as the UNESCO constitution says, "in the minds of men," and persists when men and women shrink from the age-old task of learning to resolve their conflicts. Whether we live in a forest ashram or in downtown Los Angeles, the job of being human means learning to convert our inherited tendencies from problems into positive forces. Ours is not therefore a predicament on which the experience of the past falls silent.

Schopenhauer predicted that others would soon react to the Upanishads as he had; that, in fact, the sole advantage his own enlightened century could claim over the benighted seventeenth would be its possession of those wonderful documents, which would cause a revolution in human civilization. In this, it would appear, the old pessimist was wrong. The nineteenth century and the twentieth have come and gone, and have brought neither enlightenment nor even – unless we are beginning to see it just now – the kind of open-mindedness Schopenhauer could have toward the achievements of a very different culture.

It is not that there has never been mysticism in the West. In fact, when the Western experiment with rationalism and scientific thinking began more than twenty-five hundred years ago and Greek thinkers, mainly in Asia Minor, struggled to free themselves from the mental universe of myth and symbol, the paradigm or system of thought they came up with was very like that of their Indian counterparts who had laid the basis of the Vedanta some centuries earlier. One thinks particularly of Heraclitus of Ephesus (ca. 540–475 B.C.). We remember Heraclitus for the saying "all is in flux," but he was much more excited about his discovery that underneath the flux of the phenomenal world exists *aiezoon pyr*, "everliving fire" (probably a symbol of consciousness, for which the Greeks had as yet had no single term), which ordinary human beings do not perceive but to which they owe such knowledge as they possess. This living fire that becomes all things reminds us forcibly of prana.

In a supremely important fragment Heraclitus declares, "You may search the limits of the soul without ever finding them, go down any road you will; such a profound reality it has" (Fr. 45). It would not be unfair to suggest that we have taken the scientific worldview he made possible to its very limits in the opposite direction: happiness is caused by endorphans, mother love is programmed by genes and triggered by chemicals; a full-page ad in my university's magazine recently boasted a picture of a chromosome with the heading, "This is your life." The soul has so shrunken from view that far from standing awestruck by its infinitude we have difficulty remembering that it exists: indeed, why speak of soul; mind or consciousness play no role in the electrochemical image of the human being which popular imagination and some scientists today present unchallenged.

But the time has come to challenge them. It is curious to look back from this vantage point and observe that the similarities between the founders of Western thought and the scientist-sages of the forest are so striking that from time to time Western scholars keep trying to find out whether the latter somehow influenced these "Ionian physicists" who awakened Western philosophy and science in the generation before Socrates directly.[26] Such an influence would not be unlikely. Yet at no time has the "Upanishadic" vision of a Heraclitus or an Augustine really become our own. Here the Upanishads challenge us to put in place fundamentally different concepts of who we are, and to build a life of thoughts, of personal habits, of lifestyle, of relationships, of institutions and values, and finally even of foreign policy based on the unity of consciousness rather than on the separateness of biochemical fragments.

Cultural and historical prejudices are loosening now, and that may mean we have an unparalleled opportunity to forge the kind of shift in paradigm we need to survive and grow as a united world – and perhaps Schopenhauer after all had seen this coming. In the full text of his oft-quoted remarks on the Upanishads we meet a bit of a surprise:

From every sentence deep original and sublime thoughts arise, and the whole is pervaded by a high and holy and earnest spirit. In the whole world . . . there is no study

. . . so beneficial and so elevating as that of the Upanishads. *They are destined sooner or later to become the faith of the people.*[27]

Schopenhauer foresaw not one but two major revolutions: first, that the barrier between East and West would fall, permitting a more helpful cross-cultural borrowing than had ever been the case – which, as I say, we are already beginning to see happen. But second, and even more daring, he predicted that a profound, visionary way of seeing, willing, and seeking fulfillment will become not just the thought-experiment of philosophers, as had happened at the beginning of Western scientific history, but "the faith of the people."

Of all the sources of India's vision, Schopenhauer was drawn by unerring instinct to the Upanishads. He was trying to draw our attention not to Hinduism or India, but to a habit of looking beneath the surface of life to its underlying causes, to an at-home-ness in the world with its infinite variety of creatures and natural beauty – our home and the only laboratory of our destiny – to tremendous insights into the nature of power, to a plan for world unity that seems to be embedded in every particle of reality, to a reminder that, as the Maitri Upanishad states, "One becomes like that which is in one's mind – this is the everlasting secret";[28] and most of all to the courage to discover in ourselves a higher image of the human being. These are the gifts and the challenge of the Upanishads.

END NOTES

[1] Raimundo Panikkar, *The Vedic Experience: Mantramanjari* (Berkeley and Los Angeles: University of California, 1977), p. 32 .

[2] This fortuitous translation is that of Max Müller; more on the meanings of the word *upaniṣad* below.

[3] *The Upanishads: An Anthology* (Bombay: Bharatiya Vidya Bhavan, 1970), p. 2.

[4] The translation is Panikkar's, p. 58. It should be mentioned here both that Panikkar is one of those who tends to see mysticism in the Samhitas and that book 10 of the Rig Veda, from which this hymn comes, is considered late.

[5] Rabindranath Tagore, *Sadhana* (Tucson: Omen, 1972; original ed. 1913), pp. 3–5.

[6] V. Raghavan, *The Number of Rasas* (Madras: Adyar Library, 1967), p. 34.

[7] Adin Steinsaltz, *The Essential Talmud* (New York: Basic Books, 1967), p. 4. It is interesting to note that *talmud* means "study," not unlike *veda* in the sense of "rage to know."

[8] D. S. Sarma, *The Upanishads: An Anthology* (Bombay: Bharatiya Vidya Bhavan, 1970), p. 2.

[9] E.g., Aitareya Aranyaka II.2.3.4; cp. F. Max Müller, *The Upaniṣads* (Sacred Books of the East: Oxford, 1879; Dover, 1962), vol. 1, p. 219. Early Indian commentators on Vedic texts were quite well aware of this coding and spoke of three distinct frames of reference in which the same text had often to be read: *adhibhautika,* or cosmological; *adhidaivika,* or relating to the gods, religious; and *adhyatmika,* relating to the Self.

[10] Ganganatha Jha, *The Chandogyopaniṣad* (Poona: Poona Oriental Series, Oriental Book Agency, 1942), p. 226.

[11] Cp. Müller. p. 69. This priest was said to be doing *japam,* which means reciting the sacred formulas to oneself – the same word for repetition of a name of God, or mantram as practiced today.

[12] Swami Nikhilananda, *The Māndūkyopanisad* (Mysore: Sri Ramakrisha Ashrama, 1959),p. xxxiii.

[13] R. A. Nicholson, *The Mystics of Islam* (New York: Schocken, 1975), p. 118.

[14] "We are only geometricians in regard to matter; the Greeks were first of all geometricians in the apprenticeship of virtue." Simone Weil, *The*

Iliad, A Poem of Might, in George Panichas, ed., *The Simone Weil Reader* (New York: McKay, 1977), p. 164.

[15] "Meditate on the Self, for in it all are known, as one may track an animal by its footprint" (Brihad. I.4.7; cp. also Rawson, p. 30). As Shankara states, "the only fact intended to be conveyed [by myths of creation] is realization of Atman": that is, as Gaudapada had said, the unity of existence ; cp. Swami Nikhilananda, *Māndūkyopanisad* pp. xxviif.

[16] The others are *ayam ātmā brahma,* "The Self is Brahman," *prajñānam brahma,* "Consciousness is Brahman," and *aham brahmāsmi,* "I am Brahman."

[17] On this image of food and eating, which Panikkar calls the "main image of the East," see R. Geib, "Food and Eater in Natural Philosophy of Early India," *Journal of the Oriental Institute* (Baroda) 25(1976):223–235, which cites numerous passages.

[18] Quoted in Eknath Easwaran, *Dialogue with Death: A Journey through Consciousness.* (Tomales, Calif.: Nilgiri Press, 1981, 1992) p.207.

[19] See also the later Upanishad called Muktika, "Deliverance."

[20] Note the Gita's personal version (7.11; Krishna speaking): "I am the strength in those strong ones who have dropped passion and selfish desire"; Krishna adds, "I am desire which is not contrary to dharma."

[21] Richard Falk, "Liberation from Military Logic," *Bulletin of the Atomic Scientists* 41(7):139 (August 1985).

[22] Johan Galtung, "Violence, Peace, and Peace Research," *Journal of Peace Research* 6(1969):167–191.

[23] The same is true diachronically: the Eternal Law or *sanatana dharma,* the Hindus' original name for their own religion, is expressed through moving time as the dharma of an age, and finally as *nimisha dharma,* the "law of the instant." (Cp. Plato: *chronos,* observed time, is the moving picture of *aion,* eternity.)

[24] He saw the ideal world order as a structure of "ever-widening, never-ascending circles. Life will be . . . an oceanic circle whose center will be the individual always ready to perish for the village, the latter ready to perish for the circle of villages, till at last the whole becomes one life composed of individuals, never aggressive in their arrogance, but ever humble, sharing the majesty of the oceanic circle of which they are integral units." (Prabhu and Rao, op. cit., p. 252.)

[25] Parerga II.185.

26 Cp. Martin West, *Early Greek Philosophy and the Orient* (Oxford: Clarendon, 1971), and Aurobindo, Heraclitus (10.5).

27 Radhakrishnan, op. cit., p. 17. (Emphasis added.)

28 Mait.VI. 34.3; the translation is Panikkar's, p. 422. Note the striking similarity to the opening verse of the Buddha's Dhammapada: "All that we are is the result of what we have thought," which continues, "This is an eternal law."

❶ *Glossary*

THIS BRIEF GLOSSARY IS A GUIDE only to Sanskrit terms used in this volume. Words used once and explained in context are not included. As a rough guide, Sanskrit vowels may be pronounced as in Italian or Spanish. The combinations *kh, gh, th, dh, ph,* and *bh* are always pronounced as the consonant plus a slight *h* sound: *th* as in ho*th*ead (not as in thi*ng*); *ph* as in ha*ph*azard (not as in ph*one*). Pronounce *h* as in h*ome*; *g* as in g*old*; *j* as in J*une* except in the combination *jn* (*jñ*), which can be pronounced like *gn* in Italian compa*gn*a. The other consonants are approximately as in English.

Every Sanskrit vowel has a short and a long form, the long pronounced for twice as long as the short. In English transliteration the long vowels are marked with a bar (¯). The diphthongs – *e, ai, o, au* – are also long.

The Sanskrit alphabet has 48 characters, each representing a precisely defined sound. Scholars represent these characters in our Roman alphabet by adding marks to letters as necessary, creating a system of spelling that is precise but confusing to the general reader. For simplicity, these differentiating marks have been omitted in this book, except in the introduction and the afterword when a word is used in a strictly linguistic context or within a quoted Sanskrit phrase. In all other settings *ś* and *ṣ* both appear as *sh*, the sound *ch* is so spelled, and the semivowel *ṛ* is written as *ri* – thus, for example, we write *Shiva* and *Krishna* instead of *Śiva* and *Kṛṣṇa*. Scholarly transliterations are given in brackets after the glossary entries.

Agni [*Agni*] God of fire in the Vedic pantheon, who consumes the sacrificial offering and carries it to the gods, enabling ritual communication with the divine.

ahimsa [*ahimsā*, from *a* 'not' + *himsā* 'violence']: Nonviolence; doing no injury, wishing no harm in thought, word, or deed.

akasha [*ākāśa*] Space; the subtle substrate of phenomenal reality.

ananda [*ānanda*] Pure joy, beyond the duality of pleasure and pain.

apana [*apāna*] One of the five *pranas* active in biologic functioning; controls "downward" processes such as elimination and the expenditure of sexual energy.

Aranyaka [*āraṇyaka* 'of the forest'] Third portion of each Veda, emphasizing spiritual interpretation of the Vedic rituals for those in forest retreats.

ashrama [*āśrama*] (1) Ashram, spiritual community where students live with an illumined teacher; (2) a stage of life in Hindu tradition.

asura [*asura*, taken as 'godless'] "Demon"; member of the low-

est class of creatures, the others being devas and human
beings.

Atman [*ātman* 'self'] Self; the innermost soul in every creature,
which is divine.

AUM *See* OM

Bhagavad Gita [*Bhagavat* 'Lord', *gītā* 'song'] The best known of the
Hindu scriptures, preserved as part of the *Mahabharata*
epic. It is a spiritual dialogue between Arjuna, representing
the human soul, and Sri Krishna, the supreme Self.

Bhrigu [*Bhṛgu*] Ancient sage whose legends and family line figure
prominently in the *Mahabharata* tradition.

Brahma [*Brahmā*] The Creator; in the Upanishads, a secondary
deity of the Vedic pantheon. Not to be confused with Brahman (see below).

brahmacharya [*brahmacarya* 'conduct befitting a seeker of Brahman'] Purity, complete self-control in thought, word, and
action.

Brahman [*Brahman*, from *bṛh* ' grow, expand': that which expands,
bursts into growth] The supreme Godhead, beyond all
distinctions or forms; ultimate Reality. Originally 'sacred
utterance,' and so sometimes 'the Vedas.'

Brahmana [*brāmaṇa*] The second portion of each Veda, largely
devoted to rituals; also (in this volume always written
"brahmin," as the word has come into English) a member
of the highest or priestly caste, responsible for preservation
of traditional sacred knowledge and performance of the
accompanying rites.

brahmin See under *Brahmana*.

chit [*cit*] Undifferentiated consciousness.

deva [*deva*, from *div* 'shine'] A god; one of the powers of nature or
life. In the Upanishads, the devas also sometimes stand for
human faculties or powers.

gandharva [*gandharva*] A celestial being, associated with song and
    marriage.

Gita See *Bhagavad Gita*

guna [*guṇa*] Quality; specifically, the three qualities of matter and
    energy which make up the phenomenal world: *sattva*, law,
    harmony, purity, goodness; *rajas*, energy, passion; *tamas*,
    inertia, ignorance.

Indra [*Indra*] Head of the Vedic pantheon; a sky god of Indo-Euro-
    pean origin, functionally equivalent to Zeus, Jupiter, Thor.
    Etymologically *indra* means 'power,' and in the Upanishads
    Indra is often connected with human faculties (*indriyas*,
    the organs of sense and action).

japa(m) [*japa(m)* 'repeated or uttered half audibly'] The repetition
    of a mantram or Holy Name.

karma [*karma* 'something done'] Action, work, behavior; also the
    consequences of action, spiritually and mentally as well as
    physically.

karmadeva [*karmadeva*] A celestial being, said to have become a
    god (*deva*) through right actions (*karma*).

Krishna [*Kṛṣṇa* 'dark one,' or from *kṛṣ* to attract'] After the Upani-
    shadic ages, an incarnation of Vishnu and partly historical
    figure whose teachings are preserved in the Bhagavad Gita.

kshatriya [*kṣatriya*, from *kṣatram* 'battle prowess'] Member of the
    second highest of the four castes, the warriors and rulers.

kundalini [*kuṇḍalinī* 'coiled'] Evolutionary energy; the potential
    creative power of spiritual evolution, dormant until awak-
    ened by intense spiritual disciplines.

Mahabharata [*mahābhārata* 'great epic of the Bharata clan'] Vast
    epic poem centered on the dynastic struggle between
    two factions of the descendants of Bharata, a hero whose
    name became that of India. The *Mahabharata* contains the
    Bhagavad Gita, and so much else of wisdom that it is called
    the "fifth Veda."

mahavakya [*mahāvākya* 'great utterance'] Four epigrams in the
    Upanishads considered to encapsulate their message: that
    Atman and Brahman, the Self and the Godhead, are identi-
    cal.

mantra(m) [*mantra(m)*] A quotation or verse from the Vedas, par-
    ticularly from the Samhita or hymns; also (in this volume
    spelled *mantram*) a spiritual formula consisting of or con-
    taining a name of God.

maya [*māyā*, from *mā* 'measure'] Phenomenal reality; the appear-
    ance or illusion (since Reality itself cannot be divided or
    measured) of a world of separate entities; the divine power
    which creates this world. Barely alluded to in the Upani-
    shads, maya is a key idea in the philosophical system of
    Vedanta, used to explain how the phenomenal world can be
    identical with Brahman.

moksha [*mokṣa*] Liberation (from samsara, the cycle of birth and
    rebirth), illumination, Self-realization.

nadi [*nāḍī*] A track of prana in a living creature.

O M The "unstruck sound" which can be heard in profound medita-
    tion; the Holy Word which signifies Brahman.

paramahamsa [*paramahaṃsa* 'supreme swan'] An illumined per-
    son.

parampara [*parampara*] A chain of instruction from teacher to stu-
    dent.

pitri [*pitṛ* 'father'] A departed ancestor. The pitris inhabit, or in
    a sense constitute, a blessed realm beyond this world but
    below that of the devas.

Prajapati [*Prajāpati* 'lord of creatures'] Name of the Creator.

prajna [*prajñā*, from jñā 'know'] Consciousness; transcendental
    awareness or wisdom, the highest mode of knowing. In the
    Mandukya Upanishad, *Prājña* ('of *prajñā*,' with a shift in
    vowel lengths) is the state of dreamless sleep.

prana [*prāṇa*] Vital energy, the power of life; the essential sub-

strate of all forms of energy; also one of five kinds of vital
energy in living creatures: the five pranas are *prana*, *apana*,
samana, *vyana*, and *udana*.

rajas [*rajas*] *See under* Guna.

rayi [*rayi*] Wealth; matter.

rita(m) [*ṛta(m)*] The unifying law, order, or harmony implicit in
creation; the underlying truth of life.

samadhi [*samādhi*] A state of intense concentration in which consciousness is completely unified, bringing *moksha*, illumination or Self-realization.

samana [*samāna* 'equalizing'] One of the five pranas, responsible
for harmonizing and balancing energy in the body.

Samhita [*samhitā*] The hymn (and most ancient) portions of the
four Vedas; by extension, other types of scriptural text.

samsara [*saṃsāra*] 'That which is constantly changing': the phenomenal world; the cycle of birth, death, and rebirth.

Sankhya [*sāṅkhya* 'counting'] One of the six systems of Hindu
philosophy built on the vision of the Upanishads; the cor-
responding system of practice is Yoga. Sankhya and Yoga
teach that there is an essential difference between *Purusha*,
the Self, and *prakriti*, the created world.

sannyasi [*saṇnyāsī*] A holy man, one who has taken the holy vows
of *sannyas* or renunciation (the feminine is *sannyāsinī*).

sat [*sat*] Absolute being, pure reality, the ground of existence.

sattva [*sattva*] *See under* Guna.

Shakta [*Śakta*] A worshipper of the supreme creative power
(*shakti*) of the Godhead in the Shiva tradition.

Shankara [*Śaṇkara* 'giver of peace'] A name of Shiva; a great mystic
(ca. eighth century A.D.) who rescued the Upanishads from
centuries of neglect, built on them the lofty philosophical
system called Vedanta, and established the monastic traditions which have since kept Hindu mysticism alive.

shānti [*śānti*] Perfect, transcendent peace. The Upanishads and

other sacred recitations often end with the benediction "OM
shānti shānti shānti."

Shiva [*Śiva* 'auspicious'] As Rudra, one of the most important
forms of God in the Vedic pantheon, later widely worshipped throughout Hinduism as the supreme expression
of the Godhead.

shraddha [*śraddhā*] One's central, controlling belief; usually translated "faith."

shruti [*śruti* 'heard'] Revealed wisdom, as opposed to what is
"learned" or traditional (see next entry). The Vedas, including the Upanishads, are *shruti*, revelation; all the other
sacred works of Hinduism are secondary or derivative.

smriti [*smṛti* 'memory'] Wisdom that is learned, or preserved by
tradition. Everything in Hindu spirituality after the Vedas
falls into this category, including much that is regarded as
divinely inspired.

tamas [*tamas*] *See under* Guna.

tapas [*tapas*] Heat; in the Vedas, creative ardor; austerity, control of
the senses, meditation.

tejas [*tejas*] Brightness, brilliance; spiritual radiance or splendor.

turiya [*turīya* 'fourth'] Transcendent consciousness, beyond the
states of waking, dreaming, and dreamless sleep.

udana [*udāna*, from *ud* 'up' + *an* 'breathe'] One of the five pranas, the five forms of vital energy in the body; *udana* is the
power governing the rise of spiritual energy, or *tejas*.

udgitha [*udgītha*, from *ud* 'up' + *gā* 'sing'] Important part of the
Vedic chant; by extension, in the Chandogya Upanishad,
'that which is first uttered,' i.e. OM, or the Self.

Upanishad [*upaniṣad* 'sitting down near'] A mystical text given by
illumined seers, attached to the end of one of the Vedas.

Vaishnava [*Vaiṣṇava*] Pertaining to Vishnu; belonging to his sect.

Vayu [*Vāyu*] Vedic god of wind and air.

Veda [*Veda*, from *vid* 'know'] Revealed wisdom; specifically, one of the four collections that comprise the Hindu scriptures (the Rig Veda is oldest, followed by the Sama, Atharva, and Yajur Vedas). Even more specifically, *Veda* often refers only to the most ancient part of each of these collections; see *Samhita*.

Vedanta [*vedānta*, from *veda* 'wisdom' + *anta* 'end'] (1) The "end of the Vedas": the Upanishads, both because they follow and because they consummate the rest of the Vedic material; (2) a system of philosophy based on the Upanishads, founded by Shankara, which holds that Brahman alone is ultimately real; separateness and change are only apparent distinctions superimposed on this ultimate unity.

Vishnu [*Viṣṇu*] A deity of the Vedic pantheon, later one of the most widely worshiped forms of God in Hinduism, especially in his major incarnations as Rama and Krishna.

vyana [*vyāna*] One of the five *pranas* or forms of vital energy in the body, responsible for distributing energy throughout the limbs and organs.

Vyasa [*Vyāsa*] Great sage who is the traditional compiler of the Vedas and composer of the *Mahabharata*.

yajna [*yajña*] Sacrifice, worship; self-sacrificing action, performed in service of God or as a selfless offering.

yoga [*yoga*, from *yuj* 'unite'] Union with God, Self-realization; a path or body of disciplines leading to this state; specifically, one of the six systems of Hindu philosophy, paired with the theoretical system of Sankhya.

❏⦂ *Notes*

References are to verse number

The Isha comes from the same Samhita (namely the White Yajur Veda) as the Brihadaranyaka and is traditionally associated with its colorful hero, Yajnavalkya. It is the only Upanishad to come down to us as part of a Samhita, though it has also been handed down with minor textual differences in other ways. As part of a Samhita it is entirely in verse and is today recited in the Vedic style in brahmin communities. Normally this would argue for a high antiquity for the textual form in which we have an Upanishad, but the White Yajur Veda is relatively recent.

The name too is unusual. *Īsha*, taken from the opening word, is a more personal name for God than usually occurs in the Upanishads; it is cognate with German *eigen*, "(one's) own," and means the Inner Ruler.

The language of the Isha is unusually dense and suggestive, combining mythological imagery with the most advanced mystical concepts. These notes comment on only a few of the text's suggested meanings.

[1] The opening words are *Īśā vāsyam idam sarvam*, literally "all this [the universe] is filled with the Lord." *Vāsyam* is a gerund of the root *vas*, which means "enter," "dwell with," and perhaps "put on," cognate with English "wear." The trouble is that there are five roots with this form and a gerund can have various meanings, including imperative, which the translation has not tried to convey. Max Müller translates "is to be hidden."

"All": *jagatyām jagat*, literally "all that moves in that which is cease-lessly moving"; i.e., in the phenomenal universe. *Samsāra* means the same thing.

² The text here uses mythological symbolism: literally "Set in this [the Self, Reality], Matarishvan distributes the functions" of life. Matarishvan is a little-known, somewhat Prometheus-like figure, and this primal distribution of offices, functions, and honors is a common theme in creation mythology which recurs in v. 8.

⁶ "Know no fear": *vijugupsate* is a strong word which also connotes revulsion or disgust. The sage "shrinks from none"; he or she is completely at home in the universe. As the Greeks said, "To the wise, all the world is home," and Augustine adds, "There is no saneness in those who dislike any part of creation" (*Conf.* VII.14).

⁹⁻¹⁴ This section begins simply enough: "In dark night live those for whom the world without alone is real." Then, while the structure of the thought remains one of simple polarities, the terms become unusual and pregnant with suggestion. This translation seeks to lay bare simply and clearly the basic meaning. To know Reality we must see past its dualistic forms (as the Buddhists say, "Dharma is not to be clung to; how much the less adharma"). "Nearly every chapter of the Upanishad[s]," Swami Vireswarananda points out, "begins with dualistic teaching . . . and ends with a grand flourish of Vedanta," that is, of complete monism (*Brahma-sutras*, Mayavati: Advaita Ashrama, 1948; p. lxvii). The Isha goes on to say that in practice the higher form of a duality – e.g., wisdom as opposed to ignorance, the world within as compared with the external world – is often harder to transcend than the lower. The point applies tellingly to solipsistic forms of escape such as drugs, in which one creates a private reality even more false than the apparent multiplicity of the outside world.

¹⁴ "Transcendent and immanent": *Sambhūti* and *vināśa* would seem to be the duality of becoming and passing away, or in static terms the manifest and the unmanifest. The language yields, however, an intensely suggestive paradox: "Destruction carries one free from death." Perhaps, as the Katha expounds so dramatically, when we see death – when we know the world of change for what it is – we get the motivation to escape from death permanently.

¹⁶ "That very Self am I": *so'ham asmi*, the last line of this verse, is one of the mahavakyas. "Self" in this stanza is *puruśa*, and the Sanskrit contains a striking pun: "That (*asau*) supreme Person residing in the heart of life (*asau*) am I."

⫶⫶ KATHA UPANISHAD NOTES

The Katha Upanishad belongs to the Black Yajur Veda, which had its home in the heartland of Indo-Aryan civilization, the Madhyadesha or "midland" region (today around Agra and Delhi). Of the great sage Katha after whom the Upanishad is named we learn only that he was the founder of this tradition (of which we can regard this Upanishad of his as the finest product) and a student of Vaishampayana, student of Vyasa.

As early as the Rig Veda (x.135) there is a hymn to Yama, the being who was the first to die and thus became presider over death and the dead. In this hymn a youth who has died is addressed, laments a father who has gone on before him, and tries to ride some sort of chariot – all elements which will occur in the Upanishad. Then in the Taittiriya Brahmana (III.11.8) there is a brief myth about a boy called Nachiketa to whom the god Yama reveals a certain sacrifice to be named after him. It is on this brief story that our Upanishad bases its dramatic opening. Noteworthy is that in the Brahmana, Nachiketa's third request is for the secret of *punar mrityu* or "redeath": apparently the ability to come back from death each time it occurs (which in a sense ordinary mortals do, according to the theory of reincarnation), not to go beyond death. The Upanishad, then, is not only an elaboration in length but a profound spiritual enlargement of the mythic material.

The Katha seems among the earliest verse Upanishads on grounds of meter, language, and style of thought; on the other hand it has several verses almost verbatim in common with the Bhagavad Gita and whole sections that are taken up into a later Upanishad, the Maitri. At all ages, both for India's many spiritual teachers as well as for many general readers, the Katha has been probably the most useful and popular of the Upanishads and has therefore enjoyed many translations and editions. That of Joseph Rawson (Oxford, 1934), while unfortunately out of print, is a mine of information and a very sensitive treatment (from a philosophical rather than a spiritual viewpoint). Easwaran has devoted a book to the Katha: *Dialogue With Death* (Nilgiri Press, 1981).

I . 1

² "Full of faith": literally "*śraddhā* had entered him." This crucial quality unfolds in Nachiketa in three great strides: first the seriousness with which he takes the sacrifice, next his calm response to his father's outburst that he now belongs to death, and finally his capacity to absorb Yama's great message.

⁷ These words may be spoken by Yami, Vedic Yama's consort, or by one of his attendants; *Vaivasvata* is an epithet of Yama. *Vaishvānara* (literally "everyman") is translated "like a bright flame" because it is an epithet of Agni, god of fire: Nachiketa is identified here with Agni (hence his control of the sacrifice to come) and as water placates the anger of fire, one must placate the expectation of the firelike guest who enters one's home. But its literal meaning suggests that a visitor comes as embodiment of the unity of life. "Bring water, Vaivasvata" may have been a traditional formula for such a guest ritual, so important in Indo-European societies.

⁹ Underneath the humor, Nachiketa's control over death here is quite serious. By not eating the "fruits of death" – i.e., any material thing in Yama's kingdom – he overcomes death. The theme has a mythological level also in that many heroes traveling to an otherworldly place like the land of death cannot return if they eat its food.

¹⁶⁻¹⁹ These are elements of folktale. The myth of the foundation of sacrifice, explaining how a present-day institution came about or got its name, is a classic example of etiology.

¹⁷⁻¹⁸ Yama holds out a description of what Nachiketa has won which almost makes it sound like the supreme goal. This is profound psychology, for temptations always make us feel that yielding to them will make us completely fulfilled – otherwise they would not be tempting. But Yama's last word tips his hand: Nachiketa will enjoy all this *svargaloke*, "in the world of heaven." In Hindu or Buddhist mysticism "heaven," the reward of the righteous (and earlier of the warrior), is a kind of cul-de-sac where we enjoy, but exhaust, the results of our religious or worthy secular acts and then must return to the world of spiritual progress. Only release (*moksha*), the reward of true spiritual struggle, is inexhaustible. Even Nachiketa's

achievement as the founder of a great sacrifice should not, and will not, satisfy him.

²⁵ More literally *imā rāmāḥ*, "these lovelies." Demonstrative pronouns, like the simple term *iha* "here" regularly mean "this very world" (cp. *sarvam idam*, "all this" or "the universe"). In this particular context there is a sense that Yama is almost conjuring up in Nachiketa's mind the vivid experience of sensory pleasure, more immediate and powerful than his merely seeing or even experiencing any external objects. That is probably what Yama means by offering pleasures more than worldly; i.e., they are of the world within.

²⁷ Nachiketa's singleness of purpose, his single desire, is the trait of the successful spiritual aspirant. As Ramakrishna says, if one fiber is still sticking out, the thread will not pass through the eye of the needle. Not only to desire the right thing but to unify one's desires on it is the key.

I.2

¹ Here begins the actual teaching for which Nachiketa's encounter with death has prepared us. As with Angiras's opening answer to Shaunaka (Mundaka 1.1.4), knowledge begins with discrimination, in this case between two very evocative terms: *preya*, what one is "fond" of (*priyaḥ*), often because of conditioning, and *śreya*, that which conduces to real well-being (*śrī*).

⁸ "Spiritual osmosis": Beyond words, realization is not so much taught as absorbed, as the next verse says, "from close association with a realized teacher."

¹³ This verse contains some allusive language that has been variously interpreted, without affecting the basic meaning. "Divine principle of existence" here is an adjectival form of *dharma* (it is used at the end of Gita xii as well); and the last phrase may mean "You, Nachiketa, I consider an open dwelling": i.e., open to spiritual instruction and the joy of Self-realization.

¹⁸⁻¹⁹ Very similar to Gita 2.19–20, this assurance is the basic promise of spiritual life.

²⁰ The last line of this verse has one of the few troublesome variant readings in the Upanishad. Easwaran's translation takes the text as *dhātuḥ prasādāt*, "by the grace of the Creator." Others read *dhātu*

prasādāt, "by the stilling of the constituents," i.e., the senses. It makes remarkably little difference, since divine grace consists of stilling the senses and mind. (See also next note.)

²³ Another interpretation is, "By the act of choosing the Self does one win the Self." This is equally suitable to Upanishadic teaching.

²⁵ Literally, "is curry and rice to the meal of" the Self. This is the common theme that the higher consumes the lower; as the Aitareya Aranyaka puts it, "The eater is higher than the food" (III.1.4).

1.3

¹ Literally, "Two drink rita." This image expressing the duality of human choice as between two ways of using energy (primarily our own vital energy) as two birds in one tree goes back to Rig Veda I.164.20 (where, however, it may have a different interpretation). It occurs also in the Mundaka (III.1) and Shvetashvatara (IV.6) Upanishads.

³ This famous model of human life as the conduct of a chariot recurs in the framework of the Gita, where Krishna himself drives as Arjuna's charioteer: to this day the main visual image of the Gita in popular Indian devotional art. Plato also used it, less elaborated, in the *Phaedrus*. "The roads they travel" is literally *gocarāḥ*, the senses' "cow pastures," by which they roam the phenomenal world. The term became common in Indian spiritual lore and a technical term in Sankhya philosophy.

¹⁰⁻¹¹ "The senses derive from objects of sense perception," etc.: this is precisely what the text says. As in modern physics' vision of a "participatory universe," the human mind in very real ways co-creates the outer world. This does not deny the existence of the outer world; on the other hand, as Sri Ramana Maharshi puts it without mincing words, "The heart is the center from which everything springs" (David Godman, ed., *Be As You Are: The Teachings of Sri Ramana Maharshi* [London: Arkana, 1985], p. 18). Using the modern image of the movie screen he often said, "You are the screen, the Self has created the ego, the ego has its accretions of thoughts which are displayed as the world. . . . In reality, all these are nothing but the Self. Nothing but the Self exists" (*ibid.*, p. 27).

¹⁴ This famous climax sums up, if any verse ever does, the message

of the Upanishads. It is, of course, the verse alluded to in the title of Somerset Maugham's novel *The Razor's Edge*. The imperatives ("get up," etc.) are all in the plural, and in this climactic verse the dramatic frame is allowed to slip aside, revealing that Nachiketa has really been a listener for all of us. The word which the translation (and Shankara) interprets to mean "an illumined teacher" is *varān*, "those who excel," but it also picks up *varān*, "boons," from the opening drama: "Having attained *those* desires, now strive for the lasting fulfillment of realization."

16–17 The concluding verses give traditional closure, usually of an entire text. This happens also in the Shvetashvatara, and in the loose architecture of the Upanishads it may indicate what was at some stage of the tradition an original ending.

II.1

3ff. The refrain beginning with this verse is literally *etad vai tat*, "This [very Self] is indeed That" – i.e., Brahman, the supreme, or "That which you were seeking."

12–13 This image of the Self within as "thumb-sized" is common in the Upanishads and other mystical texts, and perhaps has some background in the Vedic description of God the Creator standing "ten fingers' breadth" back from the heart (Rig x.90.1). It is an attempt to draw attention inward; the size is not to be taken literally but helps one focus all concentration within.

II.2

1 *Anuṣṭāya*, "meditates on," can also mean "governs," suiting the image of the Self as Inner Ruler of the city that is the body. Here again both meanings converge, since meditation is control, mastery.

7 The two destinations at birth cited here are probably animal ("embodied") and plant ("stationary"), the two main categories of life-forms in Indian thought. The illumined person is an exception to this law of rebirth, but all proceed, as is vividly expressed in the last line, *yathā karma, yathā śrutam*, "according to what they have done and learned."

9–10 The fire and air images end with the same formula as verse 11: the Self pervades all these forms yet remains outside all of them too.

A more literal translation would be, "As the one fire, entering the world, takes on the shape of all created things but remains outside as well," etc.

11 The word for "tainted" in this verse is *lipyate*: work done with motives of self-interest "clings to" the doer, with all the unfavorable karmic results that implies; cp. Isha 1.

15 This verse appears at Mundaka II.2.10, Gita 15.12, and elsewhere.

II.3

2 The text has "moves in prana," but the same source, Brahman, is understood.

4 This verse again shows that the belief system of Hinduism is the opposite of otherworldly or fatalistic: it places the greatest emphasis on the choices to be made in this life, in what is called *karmabhumi*, the "land of action" or "world of karma."

7-8 "Mind" (*manas*) is the seat of emotions and perception, the field of desires and other mental forces which together determine how we think and act. Its essence (here *sattvam uttamam*) is "intellect," or the highly discriminating perceptive faculty. "Ego" (here *mahān ātmā*) means the principle of differentiation by which the *jīva* or individual personality perceives itself as separate. (Later the normal term for it will be *ahamkāra*, "I-maker.") The terms used here differ somewhat from those at 1.3.10–11 (and commentators dispute their exact meanings), but roughly the same series, from the individual's mind to cosmic Mind and beyond to universal Reality, is intended.

12-13 The Upanishad is returning to the theme about spiritual teaching with which it began, that only one who has realized it can communicate it. The description of such a person here is literally *astyiti bhruvan*, "one who says, 'It *is*.'" This in turn picks up the question of Nachiketa's which started the entire inquiry: *Astyity eke*; "When someone dies, some say he *is*; others say he *is not*." The word for atheist in Sanskrit is *nāstika*, "naysayer." This affirmation acknowledges that the Self or God is the ultimate entity, depending on no other: Ramana Maharshi cited the biblical phrase "I am" as the best definition of the Self in all language, and Augustine coined an expression in Christian tradition which corresponds to what Radhakrishnan calls "rational faith in the existence of Brahman" as the first step to its realization: *Credo ut intellegam*, "I believe in order to perceive."

16 "Vital tracks": *nādīs*. "To death": literally "in every direction" other than realization.

ⅱ❙ BRIHADARANYAKA UPANISHAD NOTES

Both branches of the White Yajur Veda contain the best known of the Brahmana texts, the Shatapatha Brahmana, and within this vast storehouse of religious lore is included the Brihadaranyaka ("Great Forest" or "Great Aranyaka") Upanishad. It is much like India itself – or like another cumulative traditional text, the Mahabharata. We have selected passages to give a sense of its variety, and furnished notes to only some of them to keep within manageable size.

II.4

1 In this episode, repeated at IV.5, Yajnavalkya makes ready to enter the third traditional stage of life.

2 "My lord": *bhaga*, a term of endearment, is a less usual form of *bhagavān*, which, like the English "lord", means etymologically "sharer" or "provider." This takes on spiritual significance in the present context: "sharer of love, divine consciousness," which of course is just the role that Yajnavalkya is about to play.

3 Literally she says, "What my lord knows, let him tell." Shankara explains that what she wants to learn is (*kevalam amritavasādhanam*), "the whole body of disciplines leading to immortality."

5 Throughout this famous passage, "for [its] own sake" (etc.) renders *kāmāya*, literally "for love of" or "out of desire for." We do not really desire anything, but long for union with the Self which is in it.

6 "Confuse": the word is variously translated as "oust," "slight," or "ignore." The point is that to be fulfilled completely we must realize that everything and everyone is our very own. Wherever we sense alienation, we will not understand the universe to that extent; the expansion of our consciousness will be checked.

7-10 The illustration of the musical instruments shows that the Self is the single thread of meaning in the universe; the fire simile indicates that the entire religious culture symbolized by the fire sacrifice points back to its source, which is that same Self.

10 The word for breath literally means "out-breathing," implying that the mystic can retrace the course of evolution (as the universe does in *pralaya*, the cosmic dissolution) and be "breathed back in" to the Eternal.

12 Yajnavalkya's final aphorism is indeed confusing, as Maitreyi will indicate. He seems to mean that when the separate self which knows reality as separate and composed of perishable elements is let go of, transcended, there is no confusing knowledge (or knower) but only pure awareness. This we can never lose – it can never perish, so this is the immortality Maitreyi (who stands for every one of us) was seeking.

14 "Separateness": literally "duality, as it were" (*dvitiyam iva*). Cp. Ramana Maharshi: "There must be a duality if you are to catch hold of something else, but what *is* is only the one Self, not a duality. Hence, who is to catch hold of whom?" (David Goodman, ed., *Be As You Are: The Teachings of Sri Ramana Maharshi* (London: Arkana, 1985), p. 172).

III.4

1 Janaka was proverbially king and sage, one who enjoyed both the world and spiritual awareness. *Videha* means "without body," which may be part of the allegory of his liberation. His daughter in the bhakti tradition is Sita, consort of Sri Rama. In the Upanishad, his relationship with Yajnavalkya allegorizes the privileged relationship of a spiritual teacher to temporal authority, which to some extent still obtains in India. Their dialogues are among the most humorous in the Upanishads, as well as the most illuminating.

III.8

1 The questions of the other brahmins, which concern details of the sacrifice, have been omitted. Yajnavalkya answers his questioners masterfully, improving on whatever their previous teachers had taught them. Last to come is Gargi, the daughter of Vachaknu, who now "makes her move." "Spiritual debate": *brahmodya,* literally a "Brahman-contest."

4 "Space": *ākāśa* sometimes translated as "ether," is the nonmate-

rial substrate of the universe. Note the progression from *ākāśa* to *akṣara*, the Imperishable, in v.7.

⁸ At this point Yajnavalkya begins to "take off" and, like so many Upa-nishadic teachers, expound upon the unspoken question of the questioner: the question of human choices, destiny, and the path to immortality.

¹⁰ "Attain immortality": literally "becomes a *brāhmaṇaḥ*," which Shan-kara explains as "a knower of Brahman." A commentator, Ranga-ramanuja, adds: "From this knowing comes the attainment of im-mortality, while not knowing of it leads [one back] to *saṃsāra*."

I V. 3

This incident is recorded in the Shatapatha Brahmana, XI.6.2.10. The passage is interesting in showing the protocol controlling the pre-cious right to put questions to a spiritual teacher.

⁷ "Who is that Self?" It is difficult to convey the precise connotation of this question, *katama ātmā?* It implies that there are various selves we can identify with; which one does the sage mean? This is clearly the "takeoff point" of the episode. The self described from here on is not quite the Self but what came to be called in later tradition the *jīvātman* or the living individual's self: one's personal identity, not the absolute Self (*paramātman* or simply *ātman*) but one not attached to physical and mental forms.

⁹ In Hindu tradition *sandhya*, the "juncture" of night and day, is con-sidered an opportune time to meditate because being between both zones it is caught in neither; similarly, the term used here for the state of consciousness that is neither in this world nor beyond it is "*sandhya*, the third state, the state of sleep." Ramana Maharshi: "On whatever plane the mind happens to act, it creates a body for itself; in the physical world a physical body and in the dream world a dream body which becomes wet with dream rain and sick with dream disease" (Goodman, p. 197). The "intermediate state" can be either between waking and dreaming or between two lives.

¹¹⁻¹² The refrain which describes the Self in these verses, abbreviated in the translation, is *hiraṇmayaḥ puruṣa eka haṃsaḥ,* literally, "this golden Person, this solitary swan." There is a traditional pun on *haṃsa* ("swan") and *so'ham* ("I am He") and that splendid, solitary

bird symbolizes the absolute freedom of the Self. Yajnavalkya's use of vivid, everyday images in this section makes it one of the most effective passages in the Upanishads.

[12] "Body:" literally *avaraṃ kulāyam*, the "nest below," in keeping with the bird imagery throughout.

[21] The rare word describing freedom from desires here is *aticchanda*. Shankara comments that normally one speaks of being *svacchanda*, "able to act by one's own desire," or *paracchanda*, "forced to act by another's desire"; neither entails spiritual freedom, which is *aticchanda*, quite beyond desire altogether. The next verses repeat this logic for hearing, thinking, and so on; the translation condenses them.

[32] "But a fraction of this joy": literally *matram*, a "measure" or finite part, whereas our capacity for joy is infinite.

[33] Omitting a calculation or scale of joy very similar to Tait. II.8.

I V. 4

[1] "Powers of life": the pranas.

[5] The pregnant, simple words about desire at the end of this part contain the essential practical teaching of the Upanishads. "A person is his desire": If we can control our deep desire we can control our destiny, or the state to which one "repairs" (*abhisampadayate*). The next mantra extends the principle to the next life, as Plato does as well; cp. *Laws* 904c and the myth of Er, *Republic* 615b–end.

[7] The quoted verse is also found at Katha VI.14.

[9-23] These verses are found almost word for word in other Upanishads in this volume and are omitted here for simplicity.

[23] "This kingdom is yours": literally "You have achieved this" (i.e., the world of Brahman). To rule with detachment from selfish interest is to live in heaven on earth.

▢: CHANDOGYA UPANISHAD NOTES

Chāndogya comes from *chandoga*, the singer of the *sāman* part of the Veda, and ultimately from *chandas*, "(Vedic) song." The Upanishad is from the Sama Veda, in which the song aspect of the Samhita is emphasized. It is an early prose Upanishad.

I

1.2 Probably *rik* here stands for hymn, *sāma* for song, and *udgītha* for the impulse to sing praise. On a simpler level, most hymns of the Sama Veda come from the Rig Veda.

1.10 The word for "inner awareness" is *upaniṣad;* for "faith," *śraddhā.*

III

14.1–4 This famous brief passage of the Upanishad is known as the "Wisdom of Shandilya" (*Śandilya vidyā*). It contains a basic exposition of spiritual reality, the core of which (about our "deep desire") is repeated at Brihadaranyaka IV.4.5.

"Comes forth," etc.: all this, Shankara explains, is contained in the text's mystical word *tajjalan* (see also note on Kena IV.6).

IV

4.2 "Satyakāma Jābala": as if a patronymic, lengthening the first *a* of the mother's name to indicate "child of" and shortening the last *a* to make it masculine. *Satyakāma* means literally "lover of truth."

4.4 *Saumya* literally means possessing strength and health and possibly connotes one fit for initiation, i.e., the drinking of soma. In any case it is not a rare address and the combination of affection and respect it connotes is difficult to convey in English.

A boy seeking acceptance from a teacher would offer firewood, prostrate himself, and declare his lineage. Originally, caste gave the individual a recognizable place in the human community (as we would say today, a "network"); and it was not entirely rigid: the teacher can accept Satyakama despite his uncertain lineage, and Chandogya v.3 has a kshatriya teaching a brahmin. While the caste system had become rigid and abusive by the modern era, its original purpose was simply to recognize the differing attainments of the individual and the family's role in nurturing spiritual growth, as well as protecting the efficiency of certain divisions of labor.

V

Commentators take the bull to represent Vayu, the swan, the sun, and (more importantly) the diver bird for prana.

9.2-3 "From you alone": this touch emphasizes that there is more to spiritual instruction than mere picking up facts, however accurate; as the Katha says, truth must be caught by "spiritual osmosis" from one established in it.

V I

The translation has been simplified, omitting some philosophical arguments. As usual, what begins as a Vedic lesson becomes a platform for practical mysticism, in this case a "hands-on" experiment with energy and life. This section, with the recurring mahavakya "You are That," is considered one of the most important in the Upanishads.

8.1 The original works with a folk-etymological pun: *svapiti*, "he sleeps," from *sva* "(to him-)self" and *apīta* "gone."

V I I

1.2 The "great epic" or "traditional narrative" (*itihāsapurānam*) is the Mahabharata, said to be a storehouse of all traditional lore and often called the fifth Veda. Some of the other sciences on this interesting list are not entirely clear, but obviously this is meant to be a complete repertoire of secular and religious knowledge. Compare how Augustine (*Conf.* 1.13) complains that he was taught to "weep for Dido's death" and keep a dry eye for the fact that he himself was dying spiritually; or Faust's despair with all secular knowledge at the beginning of Goethe's play (with its very different outcome from the story of Narada).

1.4-22.1 Omitting a long list leading upwards from speech, mind, will, etc., to security, energetic activity, and happiness. At each step one must want to transcend the present step; in order to escape sorrow we must truly want happiness, or as the text says, want to know it.

25.2 The strong words used here are *svarāj* vs. *anyarāj*, freedom or "self-rule" vs. dependency or "rule of another"; see the afterword.

26.2 "Purify the mind": this could also be translated "In the purity of our nutrition (*āhāra*) lies the purity of our nature (*sattva*); in the purity of our nature lies firmness of our memory (*smriti*, meaning personal memory or tradition, i.e., culture)."

VIII

1.1-5 Omitting alternate mantras, which restate the propositions in the form of questions the knower must be prepared to answer. Note the important statement in v. 1.3 that the world within is as vast as the external world.

2.1ff. In the original this catalog is much longer.

3.2 The application of this striking image could be to our entering dreamless sleep each night or – as translated here, more universally – to our nonrecognition of the Self ever present within us.

4.1 "Bulwark": *Setur*, like *pons* in Latin, *gephyra* in Greek, originally meant an earthwork across a flooded area, and so can mean "dam" or "barrier" as well as "bridge." The text emphasizes the former meaning, but the Self or God as a bridge from our present state to infinite consciousness is also a common image (for example, Shvetashvatara VI.20). Note the later and still popular name for God, Setu Rama.

4.3 *Brahmachārya*, self-control or austerity, is the real bridge to the world of Brahman.

13.1 The demon Rahu (probably meaning "seizer"), a kind of mythological "black hole" with a habit of swallowing the sun and moon (i.e., in eclipses), stands for *asat* or *vināśa*, the force of nonbeing. The freedom of the illumined man or woman is gained when he or she is established in complete Being.

❚⁞ SHVETASHVATARA UPANISHAD NOTES

The full name of this text is *Śvetāśvatarānām mantropaniṣad*, "the verse Upanishad of the descendants of sage Shvetashvatara." No particular information is available about this family or *parampara*. The tradition is in the Taittiriya school of the Black Yajur Veda, and the Upanishad itself, despite some latish features, has always been venerated as authoritative. *Śvetāśvatara*, literally "he who has a white horse," has been traditionally interpreted as "he who has pure senses," taking *aśva* ("horse") for a symbol of the senses as in the famous chariot image at Katha 1.3.4

I

[3] "Lord of Love" here is *devātmaśakti*, literally "god-self-energy." This compound idea, characterizing the Shvetashvatara concept of Reality, is usually translated "God's own power," but a recent commentator, Swami Tyagisananda, has taken the three terms as independently meaningful (which is just as possible from the grammatical point of view) and rendered them felicitously as "the God of religion, the Self of philosophy, and the energy of science." The underlying Reality separately approached by these three human modes of knowing is seen instantly and comprehensively in the climax of meditation.

The three gunas, roughly law (or balance, harmony), energy, and inertia, whose interplay constitute the basic modalities of change in the phenomenal world according to Sankhya and other philosophical systems, are widely accepted in the background philosophic outlook of India down to the present day.

[6] Here, as elsewhere, the translation simplifies a complex Sankhya-like allegory of numbers, colors, and so on, in order to emphasize the text's essentials. "Individual self," for example, is literally *ha . msa*, "swan."

[13] At Katha 11.1.8, conversely, the birth/fire imagery (the word for the lower firestick is *yoni*, "womb") stands implicitly for spiritual "birth" or illumination. It is particularly a sacrificial fire that is thought of behind this allegory. Since it was often difficult to start the sacrificial fire with the firesticks, the priest was allowed to change places with his wife (who holds the yoni) if he got tired. This long, determined effort to bring out hidden power is a perfect symbol for the arduous work of spiritual progress: the word here is *abhyāsa*, "effort, practice," which the Gita (6.35, 12.9) calls the secret of all spiritual discipline.

I I

[1-7] This is a modernized rendering of this passage, a Vedic hymn to Savitri.

III

1 At this point the Vedic name Rudra begins to be used for the Lord. By v. 5 the adjective *śiva*, "auspicious," modifies it, and will be used six times more. In this translation it becomes a personal name – the Lord as Shiva – by verse 11, though Deussen and others would disagree.

14 This is the first verse of Rig Veda x.90, the famous creation hymn, containing the conundrum that the creative power remains "ten fingers' breadth" outside creation: the unchanged Creator is never caught in creation; the supreme Reality is both immanent in creation and transcendent. This part of the Upanishad similarly uses numerous Vedic mantras.

IV

5 A cryptic allegorical verse which the translation seeks to resolve and simplify. The text uses the words *aja* and *ajā*, masculine and feminine forms meaning both "goat" and "the unborn." Compare the better-known and clearer allegory of the two birds (iv.6, and cp. Rig Veda 1.164.20, Mundaka iii.1, Katha 1.3.1).

9 This is the verse in which *māyā* appears as the key explanation for phenomenal reality and *māyī*, "wielder of the power of illusion," as its "creator," if creation it can be called.

V

2 This verse (like v. 1.6, below) refers to the idea that wisdom – Truth – exists before phenomena are created: the Lord "bears in his thoughts and sees the fiery sage [*kapilam ṛṣim*] before creation": some have seen here a reference to Kapila, the shadowy genius who founded Sankhya.

13 Most of the language here is identical with iv.14 and its interesting reference to the unmoved, ordering Lord in the midst of chaos or our mixed reality. In this pair of concluding verses the escape from all aspects of maya just described is outlined.

VI

4 As elsewhere, the translation gives the practical interpretation of this verse. Another interpretation takes vv. 3–4 as referring to Ishvara, or God who appears to enter the world of action as an agent but remains aloof. In the Gita (3.22–23), Krishna says almost with divine tongue in cheek that while he needs absolutely nothing, he works ceaselessly to set an example to the world.

❑⦂ MUNDAKA UPANISHAD NOTES

The theme with which this Upanishad begins, the theme of higher and lower knowledge, leads to consideration of the one Reality that has become all phenomenal existence. Munda (which the Upanishad is sometimes called) means "shaved," and there may be some reference in the last two verses to a particular ascetic sect for whose members alone it was originally intended. If that was true on one level, on another level it means that those shorn of attachment to the non-self and externalities could understand its message; in fact a less well known Upanishad was called Kshurika or "Razor," and the text itself tells us that this means an instrument to cut illusion.

I . 1

[4] The words "higher" and "lower" are *para* and *apara*, literally "beyond" (or "transcendent") and "nontranscendent." Apara, "lower" knowledge, consists in the skills necessary to perform all aspects of the Vedic rites correctly. As usual, the rites stand for all human actions, arts, and skills. Para, transcendent knowing, is Self-realization.

[6] Literally "has neither *gotra* nor *varna*," social categories by which people "know" one another, and identities to which a person clings. The words have a metaphysical sense here which applies to the Self: "source and class"; but the social meaning is not lost either, relating to the personal self. *Dhīras* means both "brave, unflinching" and "wise, meditating," from the root *dhṛ*, "meditate, be firm," and is a common designation for the sages who are the sources of traditional authority.

[8] Here and in III.5 the word for meditation is *tapas*, which denotes control of the senses and mind, or "austerity," and "heat." Both suit. (See also note on Prashna 1.4.)

I.2

2-6 The translation of these verses is condensed, as the Upanishad goes into full ritual nomenclature here.

8 This stanza is found also at Katha 1.2.5.

11 The translation renders into universal terms a fairly technical description of the renunciate life of ancient India.

II.1

8 More literally, this stanza consists of a complex allegory of the sacrifice as the act of cognition.

II.2

3 *Upaniṣad* here probably stands for any text of mystical truth; thus "sacred scriptures."

4 The word translated here as "mantram" is, as usually in the Upanishads, OM.

6 "Nerves": *nāḍīs*.

9 Literally, "karma dissipates." The idea is that to live as an individual is to live tied to actions – and their results – by selfish motivations. To transcend individuality is not to be inactive, but not to be selfishly active. This liberates one completely from cause and effect. The commentaries take *parāvare*, "high and low" (our "within and without"), as referring to cause and effect: the Self includes but is beyond both.

11 This famous stanza repeats at Katha II.2.15 and elsewhere. In the world of the illumined there is no external source of awareness, nor is any needed. Likewise in the next stanza "here" (*iha*) as usual means "in this world" (of our perception).

III.1

6 "Unreality": *anṛtam*, which has the connotation of "that which is out of the rhythm" (*ṛita*) of existence.

10 Selfless desire arises as part of the world process; it is a cosmic force and cannot but work its fulfillment.

III.2

1 There is a pun on *śubhram*, the "splendor" of the source of eternal reality, and *śukram*, which means first "white, shining" and then, as here, "seed" or sperm, standing for the lure of physical life, recurring but impermanent. This is the same idea we meet in the two splendors, one a trap and one eternal, in Isha 1.6 and (with the same word, *śukram*) at Brihadaranyaka IV.3.11.

¹⁰ Though the text seems to be quoting from the Rig Veda here, the verse is not found elsewhere than the present passage. Wordplay combines the two levels of sacrifice: the seeker must sacrifice himself to *ekarṣi*, which is either the name of a certain sacrificial fire or means "one seer"; i.e., the seeker should devote himself utterly to his teacher.

❒ MANDUKYA UPANISHAD NOTES

The Mandukya is the briefest of the surviving principal Upanishads, yet it is no less ambitious than the Brihadaranyaka in scope, seeking as it does to describe the whole of reality. Extremely condensed, it was and is considered the most difficult of the Upanishads to understand accurately. Although Shankara does not mention it for some reason in his commentary on the *Brahma Sutras*, his teacher's teacher, Gaudapada, had written a 215-verse commentary which was to become one of the most influential documents of Indian philosophy, being the earliest exposition of the Vedanta we possess (and a brilliant demonstration of its validity by intellectual methods alone, independent of scriptural authority or dogma). In other ways also the Mandukya was considered a highly influential Upanishad. Like the others which center their teaching on the symbol OM, it is part of the Atharva Veda. The name would seem to come from *manduka*, "frog," as *Taittiriya* from a species of bird. A charming story was made up to explain this, but it may simply be that Mandukya was the name of the sage who composed this remarkable text.

² "This Self": Sanskrit in general uses the first person demonstrative more often than English, and the Upanishads frequently say simply "this" or "that" to mean the universe or the Self. The result is an immediacy difficult to translate: "This very Self of which the Upanishads speak, this very self is speaking . . ."

"Four states of consciousness": literally "is four-legged," an expression frequently used of the macrocosm also (the universe is said to have stood soundly on the "four legs of Brahman" at the beginning of the cycle of creation, and now is tottering on one). In the Chandogya Upanishad the student Satyakama is taught one after the other the "four feet of Brahman." But *pāda* also means "quarter" or "region," hence "the four states" of consciousness.

³ *Vaishvānara* comes from *vishva* "all" and *nara* "man"; Shankara interprets this as "he who leads all men to their enjoyments" or "the Self of all embodied beings." Literally the text refers to "the seven limbs and nineteen mouths" (one way the organs of action and perception are tallied). "Aware" is *sthūlabhuk*, "enjoying (eating) the external world."

⁴ *Taijasa* derives from *tejas*, a special term connoting the splendor of awareness, though here not the awareness of absolute Reality. It can also mean "(sex) energy."

⁵ *Prajñā* is derived from *pra*, an intensifying prefix, and *jñā*, "to know"; the meaning here is "consciousness." In dreamless sleep we are not conscious of forms or impressions; consciousness is undifferentiated, and in fact the mind and body rest, as science can detect, but the individual is not aware of it. In the next verse prajna is described as a being rather than a state: all these states are merely forms of the Self, and of the states experienced before illumination, the Self is closest to its true nature in prajna.

⁶ "Source": *yoni*, literally "womb." The language of these verses seems carefully balanced between inner (or microcosmic) and macrocosmic fields of reference.

⁷ *Turīya*, referring to the superconscious state, means literally "the Fourth." Nothing can describe it; "fourth" means only that one comes to it fourth in this anagogical order, for it is not a state of consciousness but consciousness itself, beyond the characterizable three states of waking, dreaming, and dreamless sleep.

⁸ Here the text uses an interesting expression: *adhyakshaam . . . adhimatram* means "from the point of view of the Imperishable and the measurable," respectively. The Upanishads frequently interpret the same truth *adhidaivikam* and *adhyātmikam*, "from the divine and the individual standpoints." The text conveys a mystical identity

between the states and the sounds, but the latter are to be taken as symbols, just as AUM is a symbol of the supreme Reality.

⁹ *A* is the first sound of the alphabet, and waking life the seeker's first form of experience. *A, u,* and *m* are pronounced from the throat outwards, and as the commentators say, *a* and *u* seem to merge in *m,* the closure which rounds the utterance off. A sacred recitation was always begun and ended with AUM.

¹² Literally "enters into the Self by the Self." This frequent expression hints at a great practical wisdom, developed by passages like Katha 1.2.23, "The Self can be known only by those whom the Self chooses." Buddhist teachings like "Self is the lord of self" bring the truth down to even more practical realities: self-mastery, true spiritual independence, is the first step toward Self-realization.

❏ KENA UPANISHAD NOTES

The Kena belongs to the Sama Veda, though a slightly different text of it is found in the Atharva also. It is said to belong to the Talavakara school (or *shākā*) and used to be called by that name rather than by the present one, which comes from the first word of the text.

Of more interest, perhaps, the Kena contains one of the two mysterious Upanishadic names for God which have no (or almost no) literal meaning – like *svāhā* and other ritual invocations and in accordance with the theory that Vedic mantras "have no meaning" (*anartha mantra*) other than what they are, sacred sound. The name, an answer to the opening question of the text, is *Tadvanam,* explained as coming from *tatam* and *vananīya,* meaning "the all-pervading lover" or "beloved." (The other mysterious name occurs at Chand. III.14.1.)

Unlike the Chandogya, from the same Vedic tradition, the Kena does not devote space to song or language, though the commentaries around verse 1.5 contain some of the brilliant reflections on language, especially the theory of *sphoṭa,* for which Indian philosophy is noted.

The Kena's importance has always been recognized and Shankara is said to have devoted two commentaries to it. Likewise it has been translated into many Western languages because of its clarity.

[I]

5–8 The refrain stresses, when taken more literally, that Brahman is not an object, as most people seek for it; cp. Meister Eckhart: "some people want to see God with their eyes the way they see a cow."

[II]

2 Because we know reality in a partial way and that means we know a fraction, however tiny, of Reality; but the "I" that would say "I know truth" has already committed the first blunder of knowing as a separate ego viewing reality as an object. In practical terms, whenever we think we have known the complete truth we are of course deluding ourselves.

[III]

4 The commentators point out that Fire and the others must have fallen silent in Brahman's presence, since the latter speaks first.

6 It may be meant as humorous, in the sophisticated Upanishadic context, that Agni does not mention having been humbled but only that he has not found out the being's identity.

[IV]

4 This is a striking example of the identity of macrocosm and microcosm the Upanishads often make: from the awesome flash of power in the sky to living consciousness, what we see fleetingly in the eye. Compare Augustine's famous glimpse of God in *ictu trepidantis aspectūs,* "in the striking of a fleeting look" (*Conf.* VII.17).

7 "Spiritual wisdom" is upaniṣad.

▪️ PRASHNA UPANISHAD NOTES

The Prashna or "Upanishad of the Six Questions" is one of the three classical Upanishads of the Atharva Veda. (The others are Mundaka and Mandukya.) All three place great emphasis on *pranava*, the sacred syllable AUM or OM, which has been called their "family resemblance." The Prashna is also sometimes regarded as a fuller, largely prose exposition of the prana teaching set out briefly in the Mundaka; but as the introduction indicates, it has, like each of the other Upanishads, a distinctive contribution.

Prashna, "question," is cognate with the modern German word for question, *Frage*, as well as with the German for research, *Forschung*. That is an appropriate connotation for a word describing the results of personal experience in the inner field, carried out by the mind, just as we use it for experiences in the outer field, monitored by the senses.

QUESTION I

[2] "A year": perhaps not to be taken too literally; this could mean a season of indefinite length. There are two etymological figures, incidentally: *samvatsaram samvatsyatha*, "spend a year," and *praśnān pricchatha*, "ask questions."

[4] "Meditated": the word used is again *tapas*, which means either to perform austerities or to meditate. This has unnecessarily confused some commentators, but meditation, restraining one's thoughts, is itself the most difficult austerity and the key to all the others, since it involves the most direct and systematic control of the will. (See also note on Mundaka I.1.8.)

There are two etymological figures in this mantra also: *Prajāpati prajākāma*, "the Creator desired offspring," and *tapo atapyata*, "performed meditation (or other austerities)."

[9] The two paths in the cycle of time go back to the Rig Veda. One way of looking at this, for purposes of our Upanishad, is that the moon shines by reflected light (as the intellect, in Indian philosophy, is said to shine by the reflected light of the Self); thus those who die without having realized the Self are in a state of reflected reality, while those who have realized the Self merge in Reality when the body is shed.

[11] For this verse cp. Rig Veda I.164.11–13. This is a very Indo-European image of the sun god; see Katha I.3.3 on the chariot image applied to the human being.

[13] Sex as such is not condemned by the Upanishad; rather a distinction is made in the motives, symbolized as relations at the natural time or in the daytime (and for pleasure only). Brahmacharya, as Radhakrishnan says, "is not sexual abstinence but sexual control." When sex energy is squandered, people *prāṇam . . . praskandanti*, "spill their life"; discriminatingly used, sex is *brahmacharyam eva*, "continence itself."

[16] "Pure and true": *māyā*, which might be rendered "guile" or "dissemblance," does not yet seem to connote the doctrine alluded to in the Shvetashvatara Upanishad and developed by Shankara as a key idea in Vedanta; but it may be here in germ.

QUESTION II

[2] "Body" is *bāṇa,* literally a "reed"; cp. Pascal's famous image of the human being as *un roseau pensant*, a "thinking reed."

[5] Here the "powers" praise prana as their macrocosmic equivalents (though the equivalencies are not worked out exactly). Then they go one step beyond, to Being. As the hymn progresses, its dramatic *mise-en-scène* drops out of sight until 1.12 when the powers return to view, begging prana not to leave.

QUESTION III

[5] *Apāna* is the "downward-driving force," *samāna* "the equalizing." The "seven fires" may be the seven functions listed in this verse or the seven orifices of the head: two eyes, two ears, two nostrils, the mouth.

[6] "Current": *nāḍī*, often misunderstood in this context as a physical entity and misleadingly translated as "nerve" or "vein," both of which it can also mean. The meaning here is a track of energy, to which some ascribe a causal relationship to the physical anatomy. *Vyāna* is the "distributing force" and *udāna*, discussed in the following description, "the upward." The same pair is taken as the ancestors of the sages at Atharva Veda x.7.20, in the Samhita of this Upanishad.

[10] According to this view of rebirth there is not a hairline crack for chance; we go to the destiny we have shaped by our thoughts and desires. The Gita states this same principle – that the last thoughts at death (that is, the deepest content of consciousness) will determine the next life – and adds, "Therefore remember me [Krishna] always, and struggle on" (8.7): our deepest thoughts control our destiny (Brihad. III.9.11, IV.4.5), but we can gradually shape our deepest thoughts.

QUESTION IV

[1] "Enjoys": Gargya may be referring to the bliss of dreamless sleep,

since he seems to be running through the states of consciousness (as in the Mandukya) to ask who it is who is conscious. Pippalada gets the drift of the question and answers directly.

³ An important, and complex, allegory, adumbrating the important truth our next Upanishad deals with, that human life is a sacrifice. The individual with the "fires" of prana burning within is compared to a home with its sacred hearth-fire at the center (and, in the original, with the more common image of a city) whose sacrificial altars are active when the rest sleep. Strikingly, the mind is said to perform the life-sacrifice, or to command it: *yajamāna* is the patron who pays the priests to sacrifice in his behalf. The final sacrifice, Easwaran comments, is that the mind "throws itself onto the fire" (i.e., is stilled, resorbed into prana), so that "what begins with purified butter is carried on with a purified mind."

There are many wordplays throughout this section of the Upanishad which elude translation: e.g., between *Samā* and *samāna* and between *manas* (mind) and *yajamāna*.

QUESTION V

⁶ "Awake or asleep": literally "actions outer, inner, and middle." The point is that with mind centered in the Self, an individual spontaneously acts correctly, which implies that thought and speech are spontaneously positive and in harmony. Another interpretation is that the phrase refers to thought, word, and deed. In the perspective of the Upanishads, such interpretations are not exclusive but cumulative.

QUESTION VI

¹ There may be some humor in Sukesha's elaborate attempt to cover his ignorance. On the other hand, it was serious for a brahmin not to be able to answer a ruler's question about matters for which brahmins were responsible; and the importance given to truth-telling is significant.

² *Prabhavanti*, "dwells," may mean that the sixteen forms "take independent existence." These sixteen, with some modifications, become the parts of the subtle body in Sankhya philosophy.

⁴ "Desire": *śraddhā*.

⁵ A verse form of this image is Mandukya IV.2.8. This version seems to

be arrived at by the addition of some words, one of which is important: the rivers and the parts are called respectively *samudrayānah*
and *puruṣayānah*, "sea" and "Self." (See also Chand. VIII.10.) There
is a pun throughout this section, incidentally, between *kala* "part"
and *kāla* "time, death." The words "partless" and "deathless" are ad-
jacent in the original of this mantra.

⁷ Pippalada may mean "I can say no more" or "There is no more to
be said": as the commentators point out, even incarnations of God
such as Rama cannot know the supreme Reality totally. Pippalada's
humility, if it is such, fittingly sets off his splendid answers.

⫶ TAITTIRIYA UPANISHAD NOTES

The Taittiriya tradition belongs, along with the Shvetashvatara and others, to the Black Yajur Veda. This Upanishad, which Shankara calls the
essence of the tradition, is almost entirely in prose and was originally
part of the Taittiriya Aranyaka. The name comes from that of a bird,
the *tittiri* (probably onomatopoetic), which is not unusual given Indian
reverence for all forms of life (cp. Mandukya).

PART I

¹ (Invocation). This hymn is Rig Veda I.90.9.

² These are the parts of sacred and secular speech, respectively: correct
recitation of the hymns and, with that as model, any correct act
of speech. The relationship is the same as that between ritual and
secular action.

³·¹ "We" and "us" here mean teacher and student, as in the invocation
to the Katha. "Categories" is *samhitā*, here meaning "juxtaposi-
tions," or what Baudelaire might call "correspondences."

⁵·¹ *Bhur, bhuvas, suvar*: these are the *vyāhritis*, pronounced after O M by
every brahmin at the beginning of prayers. They mean "earth, the
sky, and heaven." Along with four other sacred divisions of space
mentioned here (the translation slightly abbreviates some parts
of this Upanishad) they represent divisions of manifested reality.
Maha literally is said to *be* the Self, but statements like these should
be taken symbolically.

⁶·¹ This is one of several references to the final upward passage,

through the subtle spinal pathway, of what in the Yoga system is called *kundalini*, evolutionary energy. Before this system of spiritual psychology evolved lay the notion of *brahmarandhra*, the passageway by which the jiva leaves the body at death, identified in the physical body with the sagittal suture at the crown of the skull. (See also Brihad. IV.42.)

7.1 All vital functions come under the control of the illumined person, who identifies with the Self. As literally expressed here the statement is more cryptic: "one gains [saves] the fivefold [i.e., the five elements, external reality] by the fivefold [i.e., inner reality]"; five times five categories are listed. This idea recurs, more tersely, at the very end (III.10.6).

8.1 O M is used for "yes" in Sanskrit, not unlike *amēn* in Aramaic.

9.1 These look like nonce names: *satyavacas* means "truthsayer"; *taponitya*, "incessant self-control"; *nāka*, "heaven."

11.1–6 This famous passage is read at convocations of the Benares Hindu University. It offers good insights into the goals of ancient Indian education. As usual, it can be read on two levels; for example, "sages" is *brahmanas*, i.e., brahmins or illumined ones. Some mnemonic wordplay is used: e.g., "Give *śriyā*, "with modesty," *hriyā*, "with sympathy," and *bhiyā*, "with awe."

PART II

Though the term is not used here, the sequence of these verses follows the doctrine of the successive *kośas*, "sheaths" or "envelopes," in which the Self is encased in a human being; cp. Brihad. I.1.2.

2 The essence of food is energy, just as the essence of the earth (below, III.9) is food. (Quoted verbatim by the Maitri Upanishad, VI.12.)

6 Literally "he created what is real and what is relative, wisdom and ignorance," etc.: that is, every duality. From the Upanishads' point of view, the mode we have of knowing the sense-world is ultimately a form of ignorance.

7 Quotation of Rig Veda X.129.1, the famous creation hymn. There is wordplay here on *svayam akuruta as svakritam*, "self-made," and *sukritam*, "well made." It also makes something of a pun with *sukham*, "happiness," important for the following verses.

In one version of Shankara's comment on this passage occurs the terse assertion *bhedadarśhanam eva hi antarkaranam:* "For seeing things as separate is the sole cause of otherness." This is perhaps the most important application of the principle of participatory reality: the cause of maya, the appearance of separateness, lies in the beholder.

8.1 Cp. Katha II.3.3. The last phrase is literally "Death runs as the fifth": as it were, the Fifth Horseman of the Upanishadic apocalypse.

PART III

2 "Meditated" is conveyed strongly by an irreproducible fourfold pun (*figura etymologica*) in the original: *sa tapo 'tapyata, sa tapas taptvā,* "he meditated, having meditated this meditation."

10.5 Like the Isha and other Upanishads, the Taittiriya ends hymnally, on a note of intense spiritual emotion. The text is again somewhat cryptic, the three thrice-repeated terms in the original being "food," "eater," and "poet" (*ślokakrit*). Shankara interprets this as standing for the frequent Upanishadic hierarchy of object, subject, and consciousness beyond and embracing them. In any case, as he says, the triple repetition expresses the wonderment of illumination, a not infrequent theme in mystical literature. For the closing idea, cp. Jesus' final reassurance *egō nenīkēka ton kosmon,* "I have conquered the world." *Upaniṣad* here means both "secret meaning" and "this Upanishad."

⫶⫶ AITAREYA UPANISHAD NOTES

The Aitareya Upanishad is from the Rig Veda and forms three sections of the second part of the Aitareya Aranyaka, a continuation of the Aitareya Brahmana. In this context it shows the classic role of the Upanishads as the texts of those who, as Shankara puts it, desire freedom and thus must use the symbolism of the rites to reach a higher reality by meditation.

I. 1

2 *Ambhas* and *Apa* both signify water. The waters above and below resemble Near-Eastern creation models, and that is developed post-mythically here into something resembling the schemes of the early Ionian philosophers, particularly Thales. In the Upanishads a further step connects water as an image to the underlying substrate, consciousness. The earthly realm is called *Mara*, "death," because as Shankara puts it, death is the most important characteristic of life on earth.

[4] "Brooded": *abhyatapat*, literally "performed *tapas* over." The word occurs twice in this Upanishad and several times in the Chandogya with this meaning.

I . 2

[5] Literally "whatever offerings we make to whatever gods." No earthly undertaking, no ambition, can be free from the cycle of birth and death; but the text implies that whatever desires, hunger, or thirst we experience can be transformed (or transformed back) into desire for and devotion to the Self.

I . 3

[14] *Idamdra*: as though from *idam* "this" and *driś* "to see." With the last line one might compare Heraclitus's "The god at Delphi neither shows nor conceals; he signs" and (since Indra may stand for the natural world) Augustine's "That which is beyond vision can be seen in the visible."

II

[5] To be supernormal before birth is a common attribute of the heroes of myth and folktale; here the Upanishad again goes beyond myth by (a) defining that capacity spiritually, as profound insight, and (b) making its universal application to the potential of every human being explicit, when it artfully repeats this language at the close of the text (III.1.4).

III

[3] *Prajñānam brahma*, "Prajna is Brahman," is one of the mahavakyas. *Prajñā*, transcendent consciousness, is sometimes (less suitably) translated "intelligence." "What is moved by consciousness" (*prajñānetra*) could also mean "what has consciousness as its organ of vision" (*netra*).

⠿ MINOR UPANISHADS NOTES

The Paramahamsa Upanishad belongs to the White Yajur Veda; most other so-called minor Upanishads belong to the Atharva or have no Vedic affiliation at all. *Paramahamsa* (literally "the great or supreme swan") denotes a rare, extremely advanced mystic capable of "flying alone" in self-authority and complete freedom, like a majestic swan crossing a solitary sky. The term seems to be used here in a somewhat more technical sense than it is in the principal Upanishads. *Amrita* means "nectar"; *Tejas*, "divine splendor." *Ātmā*, of course, is *ātman*, "Self."

Tejobindu Upanishad

⁴ The three stages are *dhārana, dhyāna,* and *samādhi.* In the first, one rises above body-consciousness; in the second, the mind is so concentrated that one ceases to identify with it either. *Samadhi,* or "complete union," is more a goal than a stage, though it too is a state of consciousness in which one must learn to operate.

⁵ *Viṣṇu* literally means "(All-)pervading." Rama and Krishna are his most familiar incarnations.

Atma Upanishad

³ These stirring lines about the invulnerability of our real Self are best known from the Bhagavad Gita (2.23–24).

Amritabindu Upanishad

² *Mana eva manuṣyānām* is an etymological pun; *manu,* "human," is usually derived from *man* "to think."

¹²⁻¹³ Two traditional similes are condensed here, then set aside. A jar seems to enclose something, but the same air exists within it and without, and when the jar breaks, the air within it is released into the air to which it belonged: similarly the Self is the same in all, despite the "clay pot" of the body and the apparent differences between individuals that the body imposes.

¹⁷ The distinction is between *śabdabrahman,* or the ultimate Reality as it seems to cause, or exist in, names and forms, and *param ca yat,* "that which is beyond" phenomenal existence entirely.

[20] A pun similar to that noted above (v. 2): *manthayitavyam manasā,* "to be churned by the mind."

Paramahamsa Upanishad

[1] "Even one is enough": even one Self-realized person makes the age in which he or she lives meaningful and becomes a link in what was, in India, an uninterrupted tradition of spiritual awareness.

[2] Literally "he puts off the sacred thread" with which a brahmin boy is invested on coming into manhood. This meant renouncing the authority to perform rites: no small matter in Indian society unless one were indeed illumined.

[4] "The Lord [is] not separate from himself": literally, "His observance of the rite of *sandhya* is to draw no distinction between *jīvātman* and *paramātman*," that is, between the Self in an individual human being and the supreme Self which is identical with Brahman. *Sandhya* here means a unifying rite, one which fulfills the ritual purpose of connecting the here-and-now world with its sacred counterpart: the person who sees God in all creatures has realized completely the unity of life to which such rituals can only point. Dawn and dusk are another kind of sandhya, and considered propitious times for meditation.

"He has no need to repeat the mantram": that is, the mantram spontaneously and uninterruptedly repeats itself in his consciousness (this is called *ajapa japam*); likewise the meditative state continues uninterrupted even when such a person performs actions in the changing world (the state called *sahaja*, or "spontaneously self-generating").

◫ *Index*

OTHER BOOKS BY EKNATH EASWARAN

THE CLASSICS OF INDIAN SPIRITUALITY

Easwaran's translations, with detailed introductions explaining
the cultural background and core concepts of each scripture

THE BHAGAVAD GITA
THE DHAMMAPADA
THE UPANISHADS

THE WISDOM OF INDIA

Easwaran's personal interpretations of these three scriptures

ESSENCE OF THE BHAGAVAD GITA
A Contemporary Guide to Yoga, Meditation, & Indian Philosophy

ESSENCE OF THE DHAMMAPADA
The Buddha's Call to Nirvana

ESSENCE OF THE UPANISHADS
A Key to Indian Spirituality

THE BHAGAVAD GITA FOR DAILY LIVING

Easwaran's verse-by-verse commentary, with
stories, insights, and spiritual exercises to
bring the Gita's teachings into our own lives

Volume 1: **THE END OF SORROW** *(Chapters 1–6)*
Volume 2: **LIKE A THOUSAND SUNS** *(Chapters 7–12)*
Volume 3: **TO LOVE IS TO KNOW ME** *(Chapters 13–18)*

Nilgiri Press

Publisher's Cataloging-In-Publication Data

(Prepared by The Donohue Group, Inc.)

Upanishads. English. Selections.

    The Upanishads / introduced & translated by Eknath Easwaran ; afterword by Michael N. Nagler. -- 2nd ed.

          p.   ; cm.   -- (Classics of Indian spirituality)

    Includes bibliographic references and index.

    ISBN-13: 978-1-58638-021-2

    ISBN-10: 1-58638-021-4

I. Easwaran, Eknath.   II. Nagler, Michael N. III. Title.

BL1124.54 .E5 2007

294.5/9218   2007927661